The Nature of Ballet

A Critic's Reflections

James Monahan

PITMAN PUBLISHING

First published 1976

Pitman Publishing Ltd
Pitman House, 39 Parker Street, London, WC2B 5PB, UK

Pitman Medical Publishing Co Ltd
42 Camden Road, Tunbridge Wells, Kent, TN1 2QD, UK

Focal Press Ltd
31 Fitzroy Square, London, W1P 6BH, UK

Pitman Publishing Corporation
6 East 43rd Street, New York, NY 10017, USA

Fearon Publishers Inc
6 Davis Drive, Belmont, California 94002, USA

Pitman Publishing Pty Ltd
Pitman House, 158 Bouverie Street, Carlton, Victoria 3053,
Australia

Pitman Publishing
Copp Clark Publishing
517 Wellington Street West, Toronto, M5V 1G1, Canada

Sir Isaac Pitman and Sons Ltd
Banda Street, P O Box 46038, Nairobi, Kenya, East Africa

Pitman Publishing Co SA (Pty) Ltd
Craighall Mews, Jan Smuts Avenue, Craighall Park,
Johannesburg 2001, South Africa

© James Monahan 1976

ISBN: 0 273 00364 X

Printed in Great Britain by
Western Printing Services Ltd, Bristol
G3545:15

Preface

I saw my first ballet in November 1933 at the Alhambra, now the Odeon, in Leicester Square. The company was de Basil's and the programme *Les Sylphides*, *Les Présages* and *Beau Danube*. The dancers included Toumanova and Eglevsky (*Les Sylphides*), Baronova, Riabouchinska, Verchinina and Woizikowsky (*Les Présages*) and Massine, Danilova, Shabelevsky and, again, Baronova and Riabouchinska (*Beau Danube*). At this distance of time I cannot say that I remember much about the differences of style and personality in that first *Sylphides* of mine; what remains is a white, gauzy blur of very pretty girls against a background which, I knew later, Benois had painted 'after' Corot; but I think my memory of that evening can still identify the lines of Eglevsky's slow, lazy grace and Toumanova's adolescent beauty, so pale against the blackness of her hair, although I cannot be sure because I saw them both so often after that. I know, however, that I remember Baronova, in her wisp of crimson tunic, with Lichine in the second movement of Tchaikovsky's 'Fifth Symphony' (*Les Présages*), the imperious coquetry of Danilova in her white frills and maroon velvet skirt in *Beau Danube* and, beyond all, the lithe, taut, exquisitely timed and slightly bow-legged Hussar of Massine, a male dancer unrivalled by any in my long subsequent experience.

It would, I suppose, be possible to imagine a more bewitching introduction to the art of ballet, but not easily. I, at any rate, was bewitched and when the de Basil Company returned to London in the following summer, dancing this time at the Royal Opera House,

I was there on most nights and began to amass my 400 or so skimpy red and black folders which, in those days, were the Covent Garden programmes; a collection which, alas, vanished in the domestic convulsions caused by the events of September 1939.

Of course I might not have been bewitched by that performance in November 1933 unless I had been ready to be. The reason for my readiness was principally Arnold Haskell's *Balletomania*. That infectiously enthusiastic book, as well timed, in its way, as the fluttering hands or the snap of heels of Massine's Hussar, caught a lot of young people. It told us about the immediate, glorious past, the Diaghilevian era which had ended abruptly with the great man's death only four years earlier. But scarcely had it told us the sad news that we had missed Diaghilev and Pavlova, by so short a time, than it added that we were discovering ballet at a moment of renaissance. Diaghilev and Pavlova had gone but de Basil and the baby ballerinas had arrived. Not only that; not only were Massine and the babies breaking new ground—a rediscovery of classicism, a charm of ballet dancers younger than any professionals of the past—but the de Basil ranks were also full of talent which had proved itself under Diaghilev; and the de Basil repertory, bright with novelty, was also a treasure house of Diaghilevian ballets complete with the original designs. So not only were we coming to something new; we were being given the chance to catch up with what we had missed, though admittedly without Diaghilev's own unique touch on it. Arnold Haskell, to whom my most grateful thanks, the more significant for being so long cherished, was both historian and herald, and what he heralded was: the King is dead, long live the King.

It was, I still believe, a good moment to come to ballet. Not that things turned out quite as an eager novice expected: they never do. After a few years the de Basil Company began to break up. True, the name and a semblance of its strength remained on the other side of the Atlantic, but even before the war disintegration, through disaffection, had begun and, for European audiences, the war put paid to it. So de Basil was not really a renaissance but an epilogue. Even so, he and his did an invaluable service to ballet in London at least. The fillip he gave to enthusiasm helped our own and, I think, also the American ballet through their infancy. It might, I suppose, be argued the other way: that without de Basil the void left by the death of Diaghilev might have been filled by an even more urgent national effort. It might but I doubt it. I doubt particularly if

Ninette de Valois's enterprise at Sadler's Wells could have been use-fully expedited: her building went up fast but solidly. So that I came first to ballet at the end of one era, during which ballet had attained unprecedented distinction, and at the beginning of the next one, which was to see the flowering of the Diaghilevian seed in Britain and America (not only there but there most richly), where an indigenous ballet had never existed before. This said with due respect to Adeline Genée, the Empire Ballet and long, long before them, John Weaver, and without forgetting the altogether separate yet relevant development, since Isadora Duncan, of modern theat-rical dance in North America.

In this book I shall try to sift an experience of ballet, gathered during forty years or more, in order to put forward certain conclu-sions—how it and modern dance are kin and not kin, what it does best and less well, why ballets endure or die, which are the qualities I look for, or which have most pleased me, in dancers and, finally, where this art-form is likely to go in the near future; I am rash enough to try to look ahead, but not very far. In my first chapter I look back at the scene as it had developed before I discovered it and I say how, in my opinion, it has changed since then. So, in this chapter, I shall be making two journeys and taking the 1930s as the point of departure for both of them; the one retrospective to as far as seemed to me necessary for these reflections on the nature of ballet, the other prospective to the present time. The 1930s are my water-shed because that was when one story was in its epilogue and another was beginning; also, by starting there, I have a convenient dividing-line between the 'pre-me' past and what I have learnt mainly as a first-hand witness.

It was, very largely, Arnold Haskell who started me on these journeys. To him I have made my acknowledgement. But without the years of discussion, agreement and disagreement with my friend Mary Clarke, editor of *The Dancing Times*, I doubt if the rather long road from the 1930s would have ended in this book; and/or the book would have been a lot stupider than I hope it is. Not that she is to be blamed for any of it; not even for the views expressed by that article in *The Dancing Times* which she kindly allowed me to reprint as an Appendix. To her my affectionate, argumentative thanks.

To Gail
My dearest and unkindest critic

Contents

ONE

From Taglioni till today

I am trying to put together, not a history but some arguments about ballet as it is now and as it may become. Unless, however, the arguments are given their historical background the patient reader who persists to the later chapters may be bothered by references to which the answers would have to be sought elsewhere. That would be unfair on him. Besides, some may find that my view of ballet's present and future is quirky. The more important, then, that the book should be self-contained, providing my view, quirky or not, of the past as well.

Before Diaghilev: pre-history and the Romantics

I begin in the 1830s, the time of Marie Taglioni, *La Sylphide*, the first fruition of the 'romantic ballet', the beginning of dancing on tiptoe (on point, as it is known), the beginning, in short, of ballet as we now know it. Certainly my starting-point is arbitrary; the romantic ballet did not arrive unheralded; its seeds were germinating before Taglioni and before the great, ill-used principal choreographer of *Giselle*, Jules Perrot. Certainly it would be possible to begin a lot earlier: with Lully, Louis XIV and the foundation of the Académie Royale de la Musique, whence the Paris Opéra and the development of the French classical style as preserved for us by Rameau's *Dancing Master* and as modified, augmented and canalized by Noverre with his *ballet d'action* and by the Vestris (Gaetano), *le dieu de la danse*, and his still more deified son, Auguste; or with Didelot, the Frenchman who did so much for the Imperial Russian Ballet in St Petersburg in the early years of the 19th century—not forgetting his

3

innovation of putting the female dancers into tights. Or it would
have been possible to start earlier with the Commedia dell'Arte and
the budding, in Italy, of the stylized court-dance before it was
transplanted, across the Alps, in the French capital. But, as I have
said, this attempt to analyse current achievements, potentialities
and limitations, though historical in approach, is not another
history of ballet. So I delve into the past only to the point where
ballet, as we know it, begins to be wholly recognizable; the point
beyond which I need not (or scarcely) look for references and com-
parisons; the furthest point, too, from which the ballet we see on
stage today draws its repertory. To Sallé and Camargo I bow, re-
minding myself, happily, of Voltaire's quatrain about them, also of
Lancret's portrait of Camargo and of the other images of those
legendary rivals left to us by contemporary engravings. Madeleine
Guimard I recollect with pleasure from Boucher's portrait and from
her biography by Edmond de Goncourt. But Sallé, Camargo,
Guimard and, for that matter, Madame Theodore and the Vestris,
however alluringly they danced, are beyond the horizon of this analysis. Within that horizon the most distant figures are those of
Marie Taglioni, Fanny Elssler, Jules Perrot, Auguste Bournonville,
Carlotta Grisi, the figures of the romantic ballet.

To their predecessors, an affectionate bow—and farewell. But to
them, the romantic dancers and choreographers, our present attention. *La Sylphide*, Taglioni's signature work, is still in the repertory,
albeit not in the original version made for her by Taglioni *père*, but
in the closely contemporary one which Bournonville gave, as an
immortal gift it seems, to the Danish ballet. We even reconstruct
and put on stage Elssler's *Cachoucha* and the *grand pas de quatre*
of Taglioni, Grisi, Cerrito and Grahn; and, of course, Grisi's *Giselle*,
however transfigured since 1842 is, now even more than it was 50
years ago, one of the supreme tests which our ballerinas have to pass;
it is a test even more robustly immortal than *La Sylphide* and much
more generally compulsory.

For the purpose, then, of this essentially historical analysis, all
that precedes the romantic period can be relegated to pre-history. I
admit only one exception: *La Fille mal gardée* born in Bordeaux in
1789. An apparent rather than a genuine exception because when
it was reproduced in Paris in 1829, Hérold entirely remade its
score, with borrowings from Rossini; and the choreography was
not at all Dauberval's original of 40 years before. All that remained
was the story. And that is all that remained in the subsequent,

intermittent versions down to the, surely, enduring one made by Frederick Ashton in 1960. Still the persistence even of a ballet's scenario for nearly two centuries is not nothing; at least it says something for the kind of story, newly rustic, newly realistic, newly un-olympian, which was coming into vogue on the eve of the French revolution. So let *La Fille mal gardée* stand as a delectable exception. I am now told I must admit another half-exception: *The Whims of Cupid* (Galeotti. Copenhagen 1786). Well, yes, there it is, a little museum piece, somewhat knocked about by the museum's modern curators and occasionally exhibited by the 'Royal Danes'.

Before Diaghilev: Petipa–Baroque

In 1842, when *Giselle* was born, Paris was beyond question ballet's capital. And during the rest of the 19th century the daughter of Terpsichore, whichever daughter it may be who presides particularly over ballet, did not quite desert the Parisian shrine. We know about a succession of ballerinas at the Opéra; and there is *Coppelia*, from the 1870s, still a rung high up the ladder to be climbed by aspirants to the top, and there is, apart from what he did for *Coppelia*, Delibes's delicious music for *Sylvia*, *La Source* and other ballets which, from time to time, later choreographers (Ashton included) have used for new-old ballets; there is the music, too, of Messager (*The Two Pigeons*). Indeed, in recent years, and largely thanks to Ashton, there has been quite a revival, if not of the Parisian ballet of the latter part of the 19th century, then at least of that period's ballet music as an accompaniment to new choreography. Yet before the turn of the century ballet in Paris, where Gautier, Adam, Perrot–Coralli and Grisi once showed the world, had become a poor thing—once a princess, now a tawdry harlot. And I take as one amusing sign of this degradation, the casting of a ballerina *en travesti* as Franz, the 'hero' of *Coppelia*; a custom, by the way, which persisted at the Opéra till the 1930s. The centre had moved to Imperial Russia and particularly to St Petersburg, with Moscow, though Moscow never quite admitted this, as second best.

That statement—that Russia was a new centre—is certainly enlightened by hindsight. At the time the rising Russian eminence was not realized, even in Russia itself. If, during the second half of the century, another centre was thought to be rivalling, even outdoing Paris, that one was the traditional rival Milan and, more precisely, La Scala, where Carlo Blasis, the author of *The Code of Terpsichore*, probably the most influential textbook on ballet ever written, had been the director since 1837 and where his teaching and that of his equally famous and redoubtable successor, Enrico Cecchetti, produced some of the finest—some would say the very finest— dancers of the period. In retrospect it seems that 19th century Milan was important as a teaching centre, a maker of dancers, rather than as a maker of ballets. Virginia Zucchi and Pierina Legnani were two famous Milanese graduates; both did a long stint with the Imperial Russian ballet in St Petersburg; so did Cecchetti. They did much for the contemporary reputation of the Scala ballet but they are more significant for what they contributed to the Russian development.

Why, in that development, did pride of place belong to St Petersburg rather than Moscow? Because St Petersburg was where the Tsars lived and where the highest honours were to be won. But why Russia? In the final analysis the whys and wherefores of the migrations of an art (ballet or any other) are mysterious. Wise after the event, we put together a chain of relevant circumstances and form an explanation which more or less satisfies ourselves; but, when all is said and done, ballet, always popular in Britain, might well have taken root there in the 19th century instead of in the 20th; and there were excellent reasons why Paris might have continued to be the centre of ballet's world. Well, the Russian facts, which proved to be those which mattered most, were that the Imperial Ballet, founded in the 1730s, had been flowering gradually with the help of experts from the more sophisticated west (Didelot a memorably influential example) and also with a consistent royal support which gave it both solidity of structure and glamour. It offered a career both safe and scintillating to the under-privileged and, increasingly, it attracted talent from abroad, whether to provide fleeting visions (Taglioni, for instance) of the world's best, or to stay, as Perrot and St Léon did, for longish periods. Between them these two eminent French choreographer–ballet-masters worked in St Petersburg for nearly two decades, Perrot from 1848 to 1859 and St Léon in the 1860s. But what was to prove more significant was the arrival of another, then much less known, Frenchman, the Marseillais Marius Petipa, who came in 1847 for a year, stayed until he died in 1910 and in the meantime made 60 long ballets, countless short ones and developed a grand unprecedented style of production and choreographic virtuosity. He took ballet out of its romantic and into its high baroque period. He *was* that period. He was both a symbol of ballet's cosmopolitanism and, by his teaching as well as his choreography, the man who made specifically Russian ballet the best in the world. How voraciously this Russian ballet absorbed the foreigner! Petipa was French, the most famous of his ballerinas were the Italians, Zucchi (in *Esmeralda*, *Pharaoh's Daughter*, *Paquita*) and Legnani (in, most memorably, *Swan Lake*); the leading teachers were the French-trained Swede Christian Johanssen and, after him, the Milanese-trained Cecchetti; and the Russian style, as it evolved in Petipa's ballets was a composite of the French and Italian styles, plus Russian physique and temperament. Petipa, more than anyone, made the style. But, ironically, only about the time when his long reign was ending did Russian dancers become recognized as internationally supreme.

In one sense, he was a tree in whose shadow nothing could grow. During his 50 years in St Petersburg we hear, favourably, of no other Maryinsky choreographer apart from the wan genius, Ivanov. The second act of *Swan Lake* is both Ivanov's monument and a sign of how much more he might have left us but for the tyrannical egoism of this (by then) old master from Marseilles. But he was also a tree which, to this day, has never ceased to flower; most subsequent ballet in Russia it has been said, is either 'Petipa' or 'after Petipa'; and to ballet outside Russia he has also left a formidable and still living legacy. He raised the standard of classical ballet enormously; he consolidated that standard—and he stayed on too long. Or did he? It is true that by 1903 when he retired, aged 84, from the Imperial Theatre, he had come to epitomize the conservatism against which the new revolutionaries of the Imperial Ballet railed and struggled. True, too, that had he left the scene earlier the way might have been open sooner to new ideas in choreography and in the ancillary arts of ballet music and design. Diaghilev, Fokine and Benois might have been absorbed, might not have needed to go abroad. To lay all that at his door is unfair; he may have come to symbolize artistic conservatism but, in his later years, he was the tool rather than the arbiter of the Imperial Theatre's administrators; they, rather than he, effectively barred innovation. Besides, I wonder if the Imperial Ballet, in its artistic ideas if not in its dancing standards, would have been ready 20 or even ten years earlier for Diaghilevian revolution. Fokine was only just beginning when Petipa ended; might there have been an earlier Fokine (Ivanov perhaps) or would Diaghilev and his friends of 'The World of Art' have bypassed ballet altogether? Once you go roaming about history's might-have-beens there is no end to the fruitless fun. The facts are that as Petipa left Fokine arrived and that without Fokine Diaghilev's enterprise could not have taken the form it took.

Diaghilev: the achievement

From Taglioni, *Giselle* and Petipa, I return to Diaghilev, the story of whose Ballets Russes has been told so often and from so many personal viewpoints that its main outline may well have become blurred. Diaghilev did four things for ballet; and they could all be summed up as Emancipation and Exaltation. But, first, since I have just stressed the Imperial Ballet's conservatism during the long evening of Petipa's reign, I note that (even extreme) conservatism and atrophy are not the same thing. It is not quite true that when, in the 1890s, Diaghilev and his friends of 'The World of Art' (which was both a movement and a magazine), began to concentrate on the subject of ballet, the classical tradition in its baroque Russian form was moribund. A conservative officialdom might wish that the winds of change would not blow; they were beginning to blow all the same. Nor could a tradition be judged moribund when, in the 1880s and 1890s, it could produce the two classics, *The Sleeping Beauty* and *Swan Lake*, which have been the mainstay of the world's repertory ever since and when, helped by none of the revolutionary infusion of Diaghilev and his friends, ballet was to continue so famously from 'Tsarist' into communist Russia and for 50 years after that—and still going strong. Such was the sturdiness of the foundations laid by Petipa, the choreographer, and by Petipa, Johanssen and the other teachers. There are hard things to be said about Soviet ballet and I shall say them; but it is decidedly alive— or was until the other day—and so must have been the stock from which it grew. Yet, in Diaghilev's youth, there was rotten (balletic) wood around. *The Sleeping Beauty* and more particularly *Swan Lake* were themselves something of a revolution; the change from Minkus, Drigo and Pugni to Tchaikovsky's ballet music was a big one, too big, it seems for much of St Petersburg's conventional taste at the time. (It is fun to remember that the music of *The Sleeping Beauty* which, in 1921, when Diaghilev so sumptuously revived it in London was regarded with scorn by the orchestra, was considered too difficult by the Maryinsky's orchestra in 1885.) Petipa might be considered set in his ways but Ivanov was not and his first white, lake-side act of *Swan Lake*, though written in the accepted language, carried a romantic expressiveness which harked back to the 1830s and 1840s but was quite new to the indigenous Russian Ballet. Only fair to add that Petipa did not shun the challenge—it was he, after all, who asked Tchaikovsky to become a collaborator.

The Diaghilev revolution however, went a great deal further. It included choreography, music, decor. It made ballet dancing much more various and flexible, stretching the term 'ballet' to include kinds of dance well outside the tradition and conventions of 19th century classicism. Between 1908 and 1914 the Diaghilevian productions included an evocation of the romantic period in its purest dance form (*Les Sylphides*), a similar evocation but in highly developed *demi-caractère* (*Carnaval*), exuberant Tartar-type pyrotechnics (*Prince Igor*), an Egyptian pastiche (*Cléopâtre*), an oriental orgy (*Scheherazade*), a new, ingenious puppetry plus naturalistic crowd scenes (*Petrouchka*), an unprecedented blend of modified classicism and kaleidescopic choral dancing (*The Firebird*), a Greek-type technique (*L'Après-midi d'un Faune*), an attempt at primitive dance in a highly modern style (*Le Sacre du Printemps*)... and the list could be itemized further and extended. Instead of Minkus and Drigo, sometimes unkindly consolidated nowadays as 'Drinkus', there were Chopin, Rimsky-Korsakov, Stravinsky, Debussy, Ravel and Borodin as musical accompaniment, whether by commission —and never before had such ballet music been commissioned as *Petrouchka*, *The Firebird*, *Le Sacre* and *Daphnis and Chloe*— or by adaptation (another novelty) from existing and far from Drinkus-like scores. The conventional designs and costumes of the 19th century stage were replaced by the variety of Bakst, Benois, Roerich and, a little later, the West European masters as well. So Diaghilev enormously altered and diversified ballet in dance, music and decor. His fourth achievement was the sum of those changes, the raising of ballet to a new, unprecedented stature among the arts. An Exaltation and an Emancipation.

Diaghilev: early and late

A big distinction used to be made between Diaghilev's pre-1914 and post-Russian revolution productions; that is between the period when his Ballets Russes were new to Western Europe and when their inspiration (musical, decorative and choreographic) was predominantly Russian—between that and the later period when the

Russian revolution had severed him and his touring company from their home and when he came to rely for his material (not his choreographers and much less his dancers than his composers and designers) on what the west, particularly Paris, could provide. This distinction was made to the detriment of the latter period, when the first fine Russian frenzy had evaporated, to be replaced by a more calculated indulgence in the latest West European aesthetic fashions. The distinction remains valid, but needs to be qualified. It would be scarcely less valid to distinguish the Fokine period (1908–1912 more or less) from all that came afterwards. The period when Fokine was Diaghilev's choreographer was the Russian one (though what about the French score commissioned for Fokine's *Daphnis and Chloe* in 1911?). With the elevation of Nijinsky to choreographer and the making of *L'Après-midi* and *Le Sacre*, Diaghilev was already moving, aesthetically, from Mother Russia to a less national inspiration. So though there is no saying what Diaghilev would have done had the Russian revolution not turned him and his company into exiles, he had already started, before 1914, on the essentially Parisian, un-Russian course which he was to follow later on. In any case time, as always, has smoothed out contemporary differences; as seen from the 1970s the overall Diaghilevian achievement looks much more of a muchness.

There has been a positive revaluation as well. No longer astonished by Polovtsian dances from *Prince Igor* or Bakst's sumptuous orientalism in *Scheherazade* or Fokine's adaptation of the classical dance to more naturalistic purposes, we have tended to write-down what once seemed wonderful just because it was so new and strange, and to write-up certain works which, whatever their period, have proved to be enduringly worthwhile. This, gently and selectively, has tilted the balance; the later Diaghilev has risen, the earlier dropped a little in esteem, by the criterion of which works are considered worth seeing nowadays.

Yet the results of this revaluation must not be exaggerated. *Les Noces* (1923) it is true, is now considered the peer of anything produced by Diaghilev before 1914; *Les Biches*, Nijinska's fashionable frivolity of 1925, has its admirers again; *Le Tricorne*, if only its Spanish style can be passably captured, is a welcome revival; Balanchine's *Apollo* (1929) has become a highly regarded precursor of neo-classicism and even *Le Fils Prodigue* (1928) by the same choreographer has more life in it today than many of the once more favoured ballets by Fokine. I suppose too, that if there is one

Diaghilevian programme, more than any other except the very first of 1909, which we would all liked to have witnessed it is *The Sleeping Princess* of 1921; but that is in a category of its own, not (in 1921) a genuine novelty, however unprecedented in Western Europe, but a glorified flashback and act of homage to the Tsarist ballet of Diaghilev's youth.

Nevertheless—and putting aside this extraneous but not uncharacteristic *Sleeping Princess* of 1921—it is still the pre-1914 productions which are most frequently revived. One reason is that they are important relics; everyone, for instance, who cares about ballet has heard of *The Polovtsian Dances* and of *Scheherazade* and, if only on that account, it is worth introducing the young to them. Or they are revived because of their music; the early Stravinsky, for instance, of *The Firebird*, *Petrouchka* and *Le Sacre* lives on unquenchably in the concert-hall but it can, and repeatedly does, 'carry' a stage production as well. Besides, these three works were once sensational ballets as well as specimens of exceptionally valuable ballet music; they qualify as first-class choreographic relics.

Diaghilev: the choreographers

Yet, with one notable exception, it is not the choreography, nearly all of it by Fokine, which is the main reason why these pre-1914 Diaghilevian works are revived. The exception is *Les Sylphides*, which incidentally pre-dates every other famous or once famous work by Fokine and which, much more than incidentally, is Fokine's purest dance-ballet. *Les Sylphides* told no story at all, it was an evocation of ballet's romantic period of some 70 years before rather than an astonishing novelty, and has probably been performed more often by more companies than the rest of Fokine's choreography lumped together. Fokine's place, as a pioneer and influence, remains very prominent in the history of ballet, but he has suffered a fate not uncommon to successful pioneers: most of his choreography has become a bore and is sustained by, rather than sustains, the music and/or decor of those ballets of his which have survived. Of Diaghilev's other choreographers, Massine, exceeded only by Fokine as to the quantity of his ballets for the company, has also dwindled in reputation. That is even truer of the large amount he did, subsequently, for the de Basil Company in the 1930s. Nijinsky, as choreographer, remains a question-mark; the only surviving evidence is *L'Après-midi*, to which Jerome Robbins nearly 50 years later gave quite other choreography, much more in line with current taste—that and what Marie Rambert and others tell us about the original, lost, version of *Le Sacre*. His *Tyl Eulenspiegel* is forgotten and his choreography for *Jeux* did not greatly matter, even at the time.

Nijinska, like her brother, made few ballets but they included the memorable, rediscovered *Les Noces*. Only one, however, of the Diaghilevian choreographers has really grown in reputation; he, Balanchine, was the youngest of them and is much more famous for what he did later in the U.S. All the others did their best work for Diaghilev; but Balanchine's Diaghilevian ballets were only a prelude. Yet, whether their reputations have risen or fallen and whatever the reasons why their ballets are revived, what a team they made, these choreographers for Diaghilev—Fokine, Nijinsky, Massine, Nijinska and Balanchine! No previous period in ballet history produced such a galaxy, and all for one company. Our ballet today would be nowhere without them. Diaghilev's Ballets Russes, during the 20 years of his life, produced 82 works of which 35 have subsequently reappeared in various repertories. It is an extraordinarily high rate of survival or revival. However the credit may be allocated among Diaghilev's composers, designers and choreographers, the main credit must go to 'the brilliant charlatan' (Diaghilev's self-description) who, between 1909 and his death in 1929, raised ballet higher and made it more various than it had ever been before.

Pavlova

A word on Pavlova. She also was phenomenal and influential. From the ballets which, for the better part of two decades, she with her little company showed to the world, only her 'signature' solo, *The Dying Swan*, survives; and most of us who have seen other dancers attempt it wish they would not. What mattered was not what she danced but how and where. She toured more extensively than any dancer before or since. Though, unlike Fokine, she readily admitted a debt to Isadora Duncan and though her dancing bespoke the new freedom of 70 years ago, there was nothing *avant garde* about it or her repertory. She danced like no one before or since; there was no more and no less to it than that. Everywhere she left an indelible impression, a memory of dancing more bewitching than had been achieved by any other ballerina since or (who can tell?) including

Taglioni. Like but unlike Diaghilev she was a missionary extra-ordinary. Like him she spread the word, though much more widely than he did; unlike him the word she spread was not of emancipation and exaltation of the three united facets of ballet but simply of the enchantment of ballet dancing; yet that, of course, was also an exaltation of the art which she and Diaghilev served. She and he were not opposites; they were complementary. They were preachers who, delivering dissimilar sermons, did not always remember that they spoke for the same creed.

The new geography

So to the period covered by my own experience, from the 1930s to the 70s. The most obvious development is that ballet, previously an almost exclusively European manifestation, has spread round the world. Never before was there so much ballet in so many places. The new, widespread enthusiasm was caused largely, perhaps entirely, by the example of Diaghilev, Pavlova and the de Basil and other more ephemeral touring companies which, however inadequately, carried on where Diaghilev left off. And this enthusiasm was harnessed by the teachers, once dancers of the Maryinsky and Bolshoi, who since 1918 were exiled from Russia. It is worth remembering that, for instance, de Basil's delectable baby ballerinas, Baronova, Toumanova and Riabouchinska, all of them Russian, were trained outside Russia by one-time ballerinas of the Maryinsky, Preobrajenska among others. But, as I said earlier, this continuation, after Diaghilev, of deracinated touring companies was an epilogue and not a renaissance. The new and significant point was that the seed began to take foreign root: that national ballets began to grow where ballet previously had been a very foreign import or little more than a rumour. This, if you like, was a return to normality, though on an unprecedented scale, after the brief, gorgeous exception which was Diaghilev, because ballet, like opera and even more than a national theatre, needs a local base, a home, a school, if it is to grow and endure. Ballet needs roots. That is a rule which, admittedly, a few post-Diaghilevian companies (de Basil, Blum, de Cuevas) have circumvented, but not for long; or if, like the Festival Company, they have endured, they have not done so as leaders in ballet's new, expanding but locally rooted world. Diaghilev had not just led that world; he made it. He did it by his taste and flair, by blandishment and by defiance of the laws of financial probability. Until there is another Diaghilev, a deracinated, touring company will not do it again.

Of course, the change—the building of new homes for this quite old art—did not happen all at once. It happened because, with the dissolution of the great touring companies (Diaghilev, de Basil), more and more Russian ex-dancers set up shop as teachers, choreographers and company makers. Much the most effective of these was George Balanchine, who after Diaghilev's death was a founder member of the Basil Company; whence, leaving behind him *La Concurrence* and, prettiest of all lost ballets, *Cotillon*, he soon went to the U.S. to work with Lincoln Kirstein, to create eventually the New York City Ballet and set the American standard. And it happened because enterprising non-Russians, much influenced by the Diaghilevian example if not directly helped by ex-Diaghilevian dancers also began, on their own account, to establish new centres of ballet. So Marie Rambert and Ninette de Valois in London. So was born the Sadlers Wells, later the Royal Ballet, which became not only Britain's first ever national company but also ballet's main, new 'missionary college'. The preachers have gone out from London to Canada, Australia, South Africa, even Turkey and Iran, to spread the word which, via Diaghilev and de Basil, they had received from the Maryinsky. Only a little later than the British, the Americans too, among whom ballet has proliferated since the 1930s, have become important missionaries; for instance, they and the British between them have turned Germany into a new centre of ballet, or rather, given the highly decentralized, fragmented organization of the arts in post-war Western Germany's Federal Republic, into a multiplicity of new centres. The history of ballet has moved on. The interaction of the national and the cosmopolitan—national effort prompted by foreign influence and fostered by foreign talent— which has always characterized that history, has taken a new turn. The difference is that the scene is no longer limited to a European centre or two; it has become world-wide.

The Developing Art

There have been developments in the art itself, as distinct from its geography and its organization. A development is not necessarily an advance. In one sense there has clearly been a retreat since the time of Diaghilev. No longer do we find, nor have we found for 40 years, ballets being produced quite as a trinity (choreography, music, design) blended into a kind of transcendent unity, as used to be the rule in the productions of Diaghilev's Ballets Russes. The reason is that there has not been, and is unlikely to be for a century or so, another Diaghilev. Yes, there were exceptions under Diaghilev; by no means all his ballets were specimens of perfect 'three-in-one'; and there have been exceptions of the contrary sort in post-Diaghilevian ballets: the odd, few works in which, somehow, the unity of the three ingredients has been more or less perfectly realized. But, as to the latter, search as I may in my own experience, I can only think of two; the Fauré–Fedorovitch–Howard *La Fête Etrange* and the Franck–Fedorovitch–Ashton *Symphonic Variations*. (Incidentally, twice Fedorovitch, twice the Royal Ballet and twice music which was not written to be danced. About these prejudices, if prejudices they are, more later in chapters 3 and 4) But, then, it is arguable that Diaghilev, by raising the quality and status of the two ancillaries, the music and the decor, relatively if not absolutely depressed the status of the choreography. At all events the choreographer's situation nowadays—first not among equals but decidedly among unequals—is closer to what it was in the time of Petipa than when Fokine worked with Benois and Stravinsky, or Massine with Picasso and de Falla, under the generalship of Diaghilev. Your latter-day choreographer may not treat his composer quite as Petipa treated Tchaikovsky (even him), prescribing the exact number of bars of exactly what sort of music, but, by and large, he rules the roost. On the other hand, co-operation among the three elements which make a ballet has not gone back to the pre-Diaghilevian situation. The composition of scores, stage designs and costumes for ballet has not reverted to serfdom. Quite apart from Stravinsky, the supreme maker of ballet music for and since Diaghilev, excellent composers— excellent designers too—join nowadays in producing ballets. The top example (yet another exception) of co-operative ballet making during the past three decades has been provided by Balanchine and Stravinsky; not a Diaghilevian triumvirate under a supremo, but a diarchy to which the designer is, indeed, a mere servant but in which the choreographer does not lord it over the composer; rather the contrary. Yet, broadly, it is the choreographer who dominates ballet making nowadays; he also dominates the organization, for most ballet companies are now run by choreographers.

Choreography itself has developed in two divergent but not contradictory ways. Post-Diaghilevian choreographers, minor Petipas all of them in their dominance of ballet making, have also gone

back to Petipa-like classicism. Well, that is an over-simplification.
Fokine and Diaghilev did not desert classicism; after all *The
Sleeping Princess* of 1921 was nothing if not a tribute to Petipa;
and young Balanchine's *Apollon Musagète*, near the very end of
Diaghilev's reign, was hailed as classicism's new dawn. But the
essence of Diaghilev's and Fokine's contribution to choreography
was that it broke down the classical conventions, whereas the essence
of Ashton's and Balanchine's work, to mention only the two most
famous classicists of our time, has been a return to 'before Fokine'
—not merely a return, not merely pastiche but as they would see it
a rebuilding on undervalued and ancient foundations. Not that
Ashton and Balanchine have been very similar, but they have been
similar in this; and they have had many followers. So choreography
in our time has 'gone classical' again. But the other tendency has
been, if anything, even more conspicuous: an ever wider expansion
of classical-based choreography to encompass psychological, social,
historical drama and all sorts of styles, folkloric, national and, above
all and most recently, 'modernist' to the point where ballet at times
no longer becomes recognizable as the 'taker-over' but seems rather
to have been taken over.

Now, it is true that ballet (by which, for the moment, I mean
only classical dancing) has never been entirely unadulterated. It
was born, after all, out of social dance; it has always absorbed
national and folk dance. But that process—the refinement of various
idioms into the classical language—was so gentle, so gradual that
it bore little relation to what has been happening in our time; a
difference of degree, if you like, but so considerable as to amount to
a difference in kind. In short, the term 'ballet' has been extended
to cover such a variety of styles that it often seems impossible to
restore it to its meaning as a particular kind of dance. This is
specially relevant to its relationship with modern theatrical dance
(meaning by that the kind of unballetic, mostly barefoot dancing
which has so proliferated in the U.S.). This 'contemporary' American idiom has impregnated ballet, besides being to a lesser extent
impregnated by it, and has also set itself up as 'the Opposition': a
rival claimant to the place of honour in the world of theatrical
dance. By saying that I realize that I raise issues which have been,
are and will be hotly disputed; but, once again, let me defer argument to a later chapter (the next one). What is necessary at this
point is to enlarge a little on the subject of modern dance, to bring it,
unargumentatively, into the picture.

The moderns

Here I go back to the beginning of this century and to Isadora Duncan. That turbulent, unascetic and, in her youth, radiant phenomenon, the ardent exponent of undisciplined self-expression in movement, is usually credited with having started it all, in Europe as well as in America. She was an international harbinger of change, a symptom of impatience with academic art (not only the art of ballet), a symbol too; she was these things rather than an influence, except in the most generalized sense, on American modern dance. She taught none of its eventually famous practitioners. Perhaps she influenced Fokine; many, including her, say she did; he said she didn't but he saw her in action and though, allowing for the big difference that he abided by the essentially classical rules whereas she was an anarchy all to herself, there was an emotional if not intellectual affinity between their ends. Perhaps it was one of those coincidences which occur when the climate is right, like a scientific invention made simultaneously by un-associated experimenters. She certainly influenced Pavlova: Pavlova said so. But modern American dance's more specific impetus seems to have come from Ruth St Denis, who was an almost exact contemporary of Isadora's, and whose marriage to the almost equally well-known dancer, Ted Shawn, bred Denishawn, the name given to their collaborative enterprise. Ted Shawn, 12 years younger than his partner, presided until his death in 1972 at the annual dance festival at Jacob's Pillow in New England. Ruth St Denis taught Martha Graham and Doris Humphrey and, with these two, modern American dance really got under way. The 1920s were their formative time, when they were finding their feet and their theories. During the 1930s they blossomed; by then they had produced choreography which could not be dismissed as mere 'crack-pot new-fangledness'; they had gained a formidable apologist, John Martin, the erudite and lucid dance critic of the *New York Times*, and generally they had acquired considerable support among artistic 'progressives' in the U.S. I should add that in the 1920s and 1930s modern dance was also developing in Germany, with Mary Wigman as its most influential exponent. The Wigman influence crossed the Atlantic, in the person of Tania Holm. Kurt Jooss's *Green Table* survives, a solitary reminder of this central European modern dance, but, for the rest, it has entirely disappeared. And what modern dance there is nowadays in Germany, or anywhere in Europe, is a post-war import from the U.S.—via Britain to some extent. At the Cologne Opera House, for instance, where the permanent dance-group is 'contemporary' rather than balletic, the choreography is all American or Anglo-American or, if German, derived from Graham and her followers rather than from Wigman.

What Graham and Humphrey had in common was their revulsion from the dead, as they regarded them, academic standards of classical dance; a bundle of rules, they thought, which had lost touch with life. They were fundamentalists who wanted to get back to the basic motivations of dance. Where they differed from each other was that Humphrey was the more instinctive, Graham the more thorough, scholarly and theatrical; and those, apart from the fact that Graham, who still thrives, has long outlived Humphrey, are, I would think, the reasons why the former has been the greater of these two influences. Both had their theories. Humphrey's really amounted to the panacea of 'fall and recovery'; all physical movement, therefore all dance, rested on the interaction of balance and unbalance; and this was all the guide she needed for invention and performance. The result was that while she herself created some significant works, her legacy—the doctrine to be passed from apostle to disciple—was relatively tenuous; and her followers have become a bit scanty. The Humphrey inheritance was too intangible to endure.

Not so Graham. She had a far better sense of theatre; she was a dramatist of dance; she was almost Diaghilevian in her apt and bold use of costume and design. What mattered most, however, is that she, more than Humphrey, accepted—indeed, believed strongly in—the need for technique. Some of her pronouncements on the subject, made, admittedly, in the later, less combative years of her career, would have sounded orthodox on the lips of a ballet teacher: that technique was necessary not to limit but to free the human body's expressiveness and so on. That was why she, more than Humphrey, was able to found a school with a distinct method, communicable to pupils who in their turn became teachers of the Graham method and who, for instance, brought it across the Atlantic in the 1960s and established it pretty firmly in London. By that time, and by the same token, the followers of Graham in the U.S. were legion; or, to put it more exactly, by that time there were many American dancers and choreographers who had been schooled by Graham and had then developed their own theories of movement, their own particular 'thing', sometimes only very distantly reminiscent of the original Graham proposition although prompted by it. Among the best known of these followers of, or 'breakers-away-from', the Graham method have been Paul Taylor, Merce Cunningham, Alwin Nikolais; and there have been many others. Of course, though a Graham commandment about the need for technique might, at times, be indistinguishable from a dogma of ballet there has always been a deep difference between the two approaches to dance; by which I do not mean merely to repeat that the whole Graham 'thing' was at the outset a revulsion against ballet's corsetry. I mean that Graham's view of discipline and technique has been, by ballet's standards, extremely permissive; she has aimed at providing a basic training-in-movement and has allowed, indeed, encouraged the dancer to take it from there. The dancers, accordingly, and even more the choreographers, have taken it from there to many strange places. It would also be silly to pretend, though it is sometimes pretended, that the Graham technique, still less any derivative from it, is anything like as exacting as that of ballet. It is much less exacting; it can be acquired much later in life; and, correspondingly, it is less comprehensive. But there again I come to the threshold of argument; and argument is for later on (chapter2).

John Martin has said that the modern American dance movement ended with the death of Doris Humphrey in 1958; by then it had lost its impetus, its faith and had fossilized into technical pedantry. He may have been right, just as Graham may have been right when, some five years ago, she took exception to the sort of training which was being given, in her name, in her very own school in New York because, she thought, technique for technique's sake was taking precedence there over stimulation to self-expression. That is one horn of modern dance's dilemma: where does self-expression become not helped but throttled by discipline? But it is the other horn of the dilemma which has become much more relevant in the last two decades or so: the proliferation of self-expressiveness in dance, with little if any observable discipline at all; and, further, the development of multi-media exercises (dance mixed up with the rest) and of dance-therapeutics, dance-sociology and what not. John Martin may have been right; if so, he was consigning an ever expanding, ever more various amount of American 'dance activity' to the outer decadence.

Soviet Russian and Danish

I return from modern dance to ballet, with the reiterated reminder
that, though each has influenced the other, the former has been
essentially a revolt against the latter and has been, still is, ballet's
opposition, staking its claim to be the truer, richer, somehow more
genuine expression of the human body and the human spirit in
dance. It has challenged ballet, as folk, social and, generally,
'popular' dance never has nor ever tried to. I return to note the
Danish and Soviet ballets, both important but the latter much the
more so. The Royal Danish Ballet in Copenhagen matters because
it represents the only other tradition of classical dance which has
recognizably and at all vigorously survived—in recognizable distinction, that is, from the one which emanated from Imperial Russia
and which, put through various national sieves, has now taken root
in so many new fields. The Danish branch line, like the Russian
main one, stemmed from Paris (the Russian stemmed from Milan
as well); its distinction began 150 years ago with Auguste Bournonville and it still owes almost everything to him. I have heard a
famous Russian teacher, Volkova, implicitly disparage this
Bournonville tradition when she said that the Danes were at last
'beginning to acquire the classics', meaning by that the works of
Petipa; but, of course, the Bournonville is just as steeped in classicism as the Petipa, with the difference that it is less grand, less
given to the higher flights of virtuosity; it is cosily, neatly Danish.
But it too has shared in ballet's extensive internationalization of the
last 50 years. This may have been to its detriment, because (witness
Volkova's remark, in a sense not intended by her) it is no longer so
distinctive, so isolated in the Danish amber which kept it intact for a
century. But this has also meant that the Danish style and the
Bournonville repertory—*Napoli* and, especially, *La Sylphide*—have
begun at last to contribute their portion to the ballet of other
nations.

Soviet ballet, at least until the 1970s, was abundant evidence of
the strength of that tradition of training for ballet dancing which
was being consolidated in Imperial Russia 100 years ago. Under
the Soviet regime the standard has been vulgarized (here I refer only
to the standard of dancing, not to that of Soviet ballet as a whole),
by the change from the Imperial Maryinsky to the Communist
Kirov—a change from dancing for royalty to dancing for the
workers and, by now, for the grandchildren of the workers of the

not particularly glorious revolution. It is certainly true that, in ballet as in other things, the new, plebeian capital, Moscow, has been favoured officially and effectively over the old Imperial capital of St Petersburg/Leningrad; the Bolshoi over the Maryinsky/Kirov. The effect of this policy, over a long period now, has been to make the Bolshoi into the greater of the two world class Soviet companies; it has also blunted the edge of the stylistic difference between the one-time aristocratic delicacy of the Maryinsky/Kirov dancer and the brassiness of his or her colleague at the Bolshoi. Be that as it may; though we in the west may have strong not to say fanatical loyalty to our own dancers, the fact remains that whenever in the west, or on visits to Leningrad and Moscow, we have been able to see the best of the Bolshoi and Kirov in action, we have been stunned into submissive disloyalty. This was so when Semeyonova came to Paris in the 1930s; it has been even truer of our visions of Ulanova (late in her career), true too of Maximova, Sizova, Makarova and of several others. And if the ballerinas, though astonishing in quality and quantity, have been at least comparable with our own top-liners, the men have not been; western ballet has nothing like them. It is probable, if not provable, that Soviet training in ballet dancing, given its wider and more systematic organization, given also the ideological-nationalist prestige attached to ballet in the Soviet Union, has reached an even higher technical standard than obtained in Tsarist times. (But *cf* the Appendix.)

But there has been another side to it. Though Fokine worked, off and on, with the Maryinsky for over a decade, it was not there but under Diaghilev that his new ideas about choreography flourished and became fertile; later (much later) Soviet claims notwithstanding, he left little mark on the pre-war Imperial ballet and, correspondingly, still less on the Soviet ballet which emerged from the Tsarist ruins. As for the whole Diaghilevian concept of art, its exaltation and emancipation, Soviet ballet knew none of it. What would have happened if Diaghilev had accepted the quite pressing invitation, in the 1920s, to return to Russia? One of history's might-have-beens. But he did not accept (being Diaghilev, how could he?); and the Soviet concept of ballet continued more or less exactly where the Tsarist one left off. The pre-Fokine classics were inherited, so too the pre-Diaghilev standards of production, of music, of design. With, however, one big difference: that Tsarist ballet, though it served an aristocratic taste, was not ideological, whereas its Soviet successor was heavily ideological and 'popular'. It kept

Swan Lake but it produced *The Red Poppy* and *Flames of Paris*. It became part and parcel of socialist realism in art; and from that debasement of standards—a debasement except in the, so to say, cast-iron training of the dancers—it has never recovered. It has shared, dreadfully, in the Soviet Union's deliberate isolation from artistic developments in (particularly) Western Europe.

Ninette de Valois, after one of her earlier visits to Moscow, dismissed Soviet ballet in a characteristic phrase; 'it has no choreography'. True and untrue. True in the sense that, by western standards, Soviet choreography has never seemed more than an immutable bundle of pyrotechnical tricks perfunctorily tied together. But untrue if it implied that this unimaginative choreography could not provide a breathtaking show given the capabilities of the Soviet dancers. Nor again can we simply brush aside the capacity of Soviet ballet for heavy drama, however 'ham' it may seem to our more sophisticated taste. We may think that the combination of the two Russian exiles, Stravinsky and Balanchine, has done more for ballet than has been done by five decades of conformist Soviet choreographers and composers but it is worth remembering that Prokofiev's *Romeo and Juliet* (to say nothing of his *Cinderella*) was a Soviet ballet long before it entered the repertories of the many western companies which clamoured for it. Marvellous dancers and banal choreography—that may do as a summary of much of the ballet in Russia since the revolution; but it does not tell the whole story.

Recapitulation and prospect

I sum up. Ballet has spread world-wide during this century. Its main new centres are Britain (specifically London), the U.S. (specifically New York) and, most recently, Western Germany, chiefly Stuttgart.

Ballet as we know it was brought west from Russia during the first quarter of this century by Diaghilev and Pavlova; and the kind of ballet which Diaghilev brought was new-fangled, newly varied in style and newly exalted as to its music and designs; but its instruments were the Russian dancers trained in the Imperial Russian School.

During the second half of the 19th century ballet, or at least ballet dancing, had achieved a new proficiency in Imperial Russia. Diaghilev rebelled against this Imperial Ballet of his time, yet his whole enterprise was a product of it; and modern western ballet is, through him, derived from the Imperial Russian 'baroque period' which, in its turn, was derived from the French ballet of the romantic period and from the Italian method of training.

During the 19th century the French tradition itself did not quite die but it languished. Italy (Milan) became more important as a producer of ballet dancers if not of ballet. Yet only in Denmark did a separate, purely western line persist till our time (itself also a derivative of the Vestris style and the French romantic fashion).

Diaghilev reconverted the west to ballet. Pavlova's dancing, on her world-wide tours, was also a great stimulant. But meanwhile in Russia Diaghilev's influence was virtually unknown. Soviet ballet has carried on from the pre-Diaghilev Imperial ballet, isolated from the multitudinous developments which, in Diaghilev's time and since, have occurred in ballet elsewhere. Yet Moscow and Leningrad remain centres comparable in importance only with—some would say surpassing—New York and London.

Not only has ballet, outside Russia, enormously widened its range during this century, but a significant modern dance movement has grown up in and has spread from the U.S., influencing and being influenced by ballet, also contributing an opposition to ballet's strict academic disciplines.

This historical sketch has tried to set the present scene. In doing so it has raised a number of questions to which I deferred the answers. It is the business of the rest of this book to chase those hares, to try to give those answers. I contend that, so much having happened to and around ballet during this century, it should be possible now, as never before, to pass useful, even enduring judgements on its achievements and failures, its potentialities and its limitations. This I shall try to do.

TWO

Ballet versus the rest

A matter of definition

Once ballet was easily distinguishable. There were the five positions, the turn out of the legs and feet, the dancing on tiptoe (on point that is); there were the frilly tutus, white most often, and the tights; and, as a rule, there was an accompaniment of trivial, tuneful, obviously danceable music. That was 70 years ago, when a dictionary's definition of ballet as 'classical theatrical dancing' was, for all its brevity, inclusive and exclusive enough. Will it still do? By now there have been so many accretions to the notion of ballet, so much ivy around it, that scythe and hatchet are needed to make the tree starkly visible again uncluttered by parasites. But is that metaphor valid any more? It ignores the fact that language develops and that words change their meaning because, among other reasons, the objects described by the words have themselves changed. What is to be made of 'Ballets Nègres', 'Burmese Ballet', 'Ballet of India', 'Folklore Ballet' and, particularly, the various modern-style 'ballet' companies whose forms of dance have nothing to do with Europe's classical, theatrical dancing? For that matter, what about Britain's oldest company, the Rambert, once as classical as anything but now so largely devoted to modern idioms that, if the traditional definition is to be maintained, the title of the 'Ballet Rambert' has become an anachronism?

Confusion is made more confusing because the term is used in two related but separate senses, each of which can be vague. It is used both for the group of performers ('les Ballets Russes') and for what they perform ('Ballet Imperial'). That did not matter so long as the group's title bespoke the kind of performance. But that is no longer so, when not only can 'ballet' be in the title of a group which performs nothing classical at all but also the repertory of a 'ballet' company may contain some items which are wholly classical, others which are wholly unclassical and yet others which are a mixture. Just what proportion of classical to unclassical in a given work or, overall, in a repertory, should warrant 'ballet' in the title of the work or of the performing group? It is, of course, impossible to say. Does it matter? I very much like terminological exactitude— yes, for its own sake—but here I am not concerned with that. I am concerned only with clarity, and with that only so far as it is required to avoid vexatious muddle and a plethora of explanations. So the questions reduce to this one: is it worth undertaking a rescue operation to restore the term 'ballet' to its pristine meaning? The answer is a qualified 'yes'. It has to be qualified because it really is no use trying to sort out how much classical dancing in a given work or repertory should authorize that work, or the company using that repertory, to be titled with 'ballet'; there is no stopping— no one would want to stop—the Rambert from continuing to wear 'Ballet Rambert' as its hat. But the answer is 'yes' all the same, because it has become more necessary, not less, in these times of inexact nomenclature to insist that there remains a distinction among styles of dance. A kind of thinking prevails which is summed up in the cosy observation that 'the type of choreography doesn't matter; all that matters is that it should be good'. An obviously true statement, you may say; so obviously true that it is not worth making. I attack it. I do so because it implies that any kind of dancer may produce results as good or as bad as those pro- duced by any other, that there is nothing to choose between styles in themselves, that technique, and which technique, does not matter. I attack it because it, or the spirit behind it, is conducive to mush and muddle. So, due allowance being made for anachron- istic titles and, no doubt, for other exceptions, the term 'ballet' should only be applied to the element of classical theatrical dancing in a particular work or repertory, no matter if it is mixed with other elements; to that and to companies or individuals who predomin- antly specialize in such dancing. Having said that, I do not say that in this book the term is used only in that exact sense. But where, for brevity's sake, it is used otherwise the distinction, between ballet and the rest, is neither relevant nor jeopardized. That assurance I give, however brashly.

Three differences

The distinction is in the technique. By which apparent platitude I mean three things. I mean, first, that the technique of ballet dancing is particularly hard to acquire. As I said earlier it takes much longer to become proficient in ballet than in any other kind of occidental dance. Some good male dancers have started only in their teens; but most, including nearly all the best, begin before they are 12. As for the girls, with their extra and extraordinary task of dancing on point, very few indeed who started later than eight or nine have become good dancers. (The marvellously, naturally 'turned out' Jennifer Penney is, infuriatingly, one of the very few. She started, I believe, at thirteen.) I mean that the technique of ballet is exceptional artificial, stylized to an exceptionally high degree. That is not to say that its technique eschews naturalism altogether; there are postures, gestures, movements in ballet which are not unnatural but only unusual—a really erect carriage, for instance, the well hollowed back, the weight of the body not slumping but 'pulled up'. That, incidentally, is why it can be excellently remedial, up to a point; it can teach how to move, stand and sit not as most people do but as they should. In so far as it is natural it is naturalism idealized. But, as to its most characteristic aspects—the turn out and, for the girls, the dancing on point—it is clearly not natural and though the acquisition of these techniques brings a healthy increase of strength it also imposes unnatural strain. And my third meaning is that the technique of ballet, in its idealized naturalism and its unnaturalness, is concerned with many things—neatness, grandeur, delicacy, speed of movement, balance, lightness, an ability not just to jump but to seem to soar, line and general virtuosity—but of all these the primary objectives are lightness and line. There have been good, even great, ballet dancers who could not jump much but there was never a good one, still less a great one who, whether or not he or she really was a remarkable jumper, did not give an impression of lightness. There was never one admired for seeming heavy. Lightness is not quite synonymous with concealment of effort, but the two are very close kin.

Line

Line is wholly concerned with the shape, the pattern, of a dancer, or two dancers or a group of them, as seen by the audience; and this —to achieve good line as seen by the audience—is the particular though not the exclusive purpose of ballet's most characteristic artificialities, the turn out, plus the arched foot and pointed toe. Good line and symmetry are, again, not synonymous, but again, they are closely related. Nevertheless, the intended visual effect may well be, may be more often than not, assymetrical; the aim may sometimes be discord rather than harmony. Is there an absolute goodness of line? I think that, ultimately and ideally, there is. At the more workaday level, of an audience's judgement as to whether or not a dancer's line is good, there is certainly a lot of agreement; no one, for instance, has denied that the purity of Fonteyn's line is one of the main reasons why she has been a great dancer. Not that disagreement about the quality of a dancer's line can be ruled out, any more than unanimity can be expected about the linear merit of a painting, drawing, sculpture or building or, in the broadest sense, any visible design. Nor, of course, is good line a thing of chance; physical proportions matter greatly but, after that, it is a matter of sedulously training the physique to form patterns which (this I emphasize) will look good from the theatre's auditorium. What then is it? It is a linear harmony and/or constrast of the positions of fingers, wrists, arms, head, torso, legs and feet. We may think usually of the best line as being the most graceful; so, in classical dance, it is, but it is not necessarily so. It must be expressive too; and the required line for an Odette–Odile or Aurora is, indeed, graceful but quite other patterns, a quite other expressiveness of line, may be required in a modern ballet. It is, I repeat, the pattern as seen across the footlights that counts. The whole body contributes to it, but the most conspicuous contributors are those most extreme artificialities or stylizations in ballet training—the turn out, the arched foot, the pointed toe; not only these, but these most distinctively produce good line. And if it is true that the line which ballet training tries to produce is the classical, traditional one of an Odette–Odile or Aurora, it is also true that training in ballet is meant to, and does, make a highly adaptable instrument.

An adaptable instrument

The ballet dancer as instrument, ballet dancing as communication across the footlights; these are separate concepts but they are linked. There is an apparent paradox, if not contradiction, about training in ballet; the end product of its artificialities, its stylization, is a highly specialized kind of performance; on the other hand the claim is made that a dancer trained in ballet is more adaptable than any other. A just claim in my view. The common sense of it is that this training is so exacting that the adaptation of a ballet trained body to other kinds of dancing—and I am thinking mainly of the modern types—is relatively easy, whereas it is quite impossible for dancers formed in another mould to adapt themselves to ballet. The 'turned out' ballet dancer has no insuperable difficulty in being 'turned in' if the choreography so requires; but the 'turned in' dancer cannot return the compliment. That is what I mean by saying that of all dancers the ballet trained one is the most adaptable instrument: an instrument for communicating choreography to an audience. And usually the choreography will be that of someone other than the dancer. But—I hear the immediate protest—is not that common to all dance of any kind which people pay to watch? Not quite so. My point here is to emphasize the outwardness of ballet, the fact that it is wholly and entirely for an audience's enjoyment, not for the private pleasure, the self-expression of dancer and choreographer.

Self-expression and discipline

That is where issue is joined between ballet and 'contemporary' dance. In practice the issue is not so stark as that. The choice, in practice, is not between wholly outward-looking ballet, only concerned, like the most frankly commercial 'musical comedy' kind of dance, with making a show, and inward-looking modern dance concerned wholly with private devotions. The two merge: Martha Graham is a communicator, intent on theatrical values; Pavlova, as dancer-choreographer, and Balanchine and Ashton, as choreographers, have been nothing if not self-expressionists. The two merge because people, when it comes to doing and making, are not, thank goodness, the slaves of their theories. Yet the theories matter; and the basic distinction between ballet and modern dance in their approaches to their subject remains valid and significant. It is the difference between a comprehensive discipline adaptable to other idioms of dance and capable of a wide range of expressiveness —between that and a devotion to self-expression which is content with a less exacting, less comprehensive discipline. It is the difference, again, between a classical and a romantic attitude. Or—which some would say was very nearly saying the same thing—the difference between those who give first priority to form and those whose first priorities are 'feeling' and perhaps 'meaning' too. But is that quite so? Is the simple distinction between ballet as representing form and modern dance as representing meaning and feeling in dance to be accepted just like that? Modernists, or many of them, would answer 'yes' and would add that this is what the modern dance movement is all about: a revolt from the formalistic emptiness of ballet in favour of meaningful or at least genuinely 'feeling-full' self-expression. But the right answer is more complicated.

Romantic–Classical

Take as starting-point the romantic–classical distinction, that old familiar of the story of art, any art. This age of the hydrogen bomb is, surprisingly or not, a romantic age. Narrowing it down to dance, what this means is that it is an age of extreme impatience with tradition, an age in which every choreographer or dancer (well almost every one of them) wishes to do his or her thing—and away with the inherited disciplines. Sure enough this impulse can be traced back to Isadora Duncan, and that was long before the atomic or hydrogen bomb; so, come to that, were Martha Graham and Doris Humphrey, when in the 1920s they began to codify this impulse. In the post-second world war period, however, the process has become enormously accelerated.

In my introductory recapitulation of dance history I hinted at the difficulties, the misunderstandings inherent in the terms 'romantic' and 'classical' as applied to ballet. Romantic and classical are usually taken to be opposites and yet I took the romantic period, of some 140 years ago, as being the one during which classical ballet, as we now know it, becomes recognizable. The self-contradiction is only apparent, not real, the point being that, in dance at least, the romantic movement of the early 19th century was within the classical framework; it belonged to the classical tradition's evolution. The difference nowadays is that, in dance, our modern romantic movement is so largely, or at least so vociferously, not inside but right outside the tradition. That pretty downright statement having been made, the qualifications immediately begin (so it is always in any attempt to categorize, to itemize the development of any art). True that dance's modern romantic movement can be traced from Isadora to Graham, to Merce Cunningham and to whatever 'ultra' you care to think of, but also true that Fokine, influenced or not by Isadora, belonged to this romantic movement—with the enormous difference that he and his Diaghilevian and post-Diaghilevian successors stayed within the tradition. How, again, is that compatible with what I said, in my first chapter, about the emancipation of ballet under and since Diaghilev so as to include, within a ballet company's repertory, all sorts of dance idioms which had little or nothing to do with the classical tradition? How—to take examples only from the earlier pre-1914 Diaghilev seasons—can it be reconciled with the 'Hellenic' style of Nijinsky's *L'Apres-midi* or with his *Sacre du Printemps* for which the dancers needed coaching by the young Dalcroze-trained Marie Rambert? Qualification within qualification. The fact is that some Diaghilevian choreography and much more in the repertories of post-Diaghilevian ballet companies, did go and does go right outside the tradition; and it could not be maintained that for all this deviationist choreography (the term being used unpejoratively) ballet trained dancers were or are necessary. The classical concept becomes meaningless if you stretch it to include everything that is performed by ballet trained dancers; on the other hand, their training does maintain the tradition and so does a great deal of what they are required to perform.

The two kinds of badness

If there is a badness which is characteristic of bad classical choreography it is, beyond doubt, an empty formalism: an embroidery of insignificant, academic movements. And the characteristics of bad 'contemporary' choreography are a shapelessness, a mess of movements which are, allegedly, meant to express deep feelings and perhaps deep meanings too. Those are the extremes; and I daresay that in their different ways they are equally reprehensible; that is, unless characteristically bad classical choreography were taken, as it might be, to include sheer virtuosity, those loosely tied bundles, for instance, of more or less academic pyrotechnics which the Russians go in for and which, as I mentioned earlier, Ninette de Valois for one has described as 'non-choreography'. We may sniff at such pyrotechnics as inartistic, soulless, vulgar, but the sniffs are apt to be unpersuasive. Sheer virtuosity, however vulgar, can be irresistible—and forget about its artistic vacuity. In fact, I do not think that the choreography, however vulgar, of a dazzling performance can be described as downright bad; it may be a distortion, a caricature, of one of the purposes of ballet training, but nevertheless a positive one; a way of pleasing an audience which belongs to this technique and much less to any other. Such virtuosity, you might say, is the joker in ballet's pack. But the kind of badness which I have in mind as being characteristic of bad balletic choreography is not like that; it is just the dull stuff of unimaginative academic correctness.

The way to progress

If, then, there is no choosing between the louse of bad classical and the flea of bad modern choreography it does not, of course, follow that the balance is equally nice as between classical and modern type choreography in general. There remains the great difference in range or, to put it another way, in power to absorb, to adapt. What it comes to is that the formalized, stylized technique, because it is much the more exacting, can take in a lot that is more or less extraneous to it; the more limited technique can take in much less. And, to carry this train of thought a little further, it means too that the ultimate value of the romantic impulse, as manifested in dance, is in what classicism can absorb, adapt from it; that rather than the other way round. Romantic, 'contemporary' dance cannot really begin to absorb classicism; its technical means are too frail, too shallow. And when John Martin, the eminent American critic who has been so strenuous and so devoted an apologist for modern American dance, said that the modern movement died with Doris Humphrey in 1958, this was his implication: that the movement's coherent vitality was being, on the one hand, fragmented into ever more private romantic shreds and, on the other, was hardening into a fossilized discipline. This was tantamount to saying that, in the nature of things, the modern movement—any movement which represented a breakaway from the tradition rather than an attempt to modify the tradition from within—was bound to be short-lived. Tantamount also to admitting that there is a built-in self-contradiction even in Martha Graham's dance philosophy; and I stress Graham, not only because she has been much the most influential modernist but because she has seen the problem more clearly than any of them. Seen it but, inevitably, been unable to solve it. For if the motivation is untrammelled self-expression—and away with the inherited disciplines—but at the same time it is recognized that without discipline, without training, self-expression in dance becomes a footling, uncommunicative self-indulgence, which way can progress lie? The answer is: neither way. So in my experience it has proved. But there is another answer, the only right one in my view: that, first of all, it has to be recognized that undisciplined self-expression does, indeed lead quickly nowhere (no argument about that) and, next, that since discipline there must be, then the discipline to go for, the one which will pay long-term dividends, is not a kind of minimal compromise but a whole-hogging, tough and comprehensive one. The answer can only be in the discipline which is most thorough and most comprehensive. I do not say that this must be true always everywhere; only that it is incontrovertibly so in western dance as it has been, is and predictably will be.

Meaning versus movement-quality

Here another self-contradiction becomes relevant: one about the meaning of dance. I have labelled the modern movement in dance as romantic ('breakaway' romantic as distinct from romantic within the classical tradition) and I have ascribed to it an emphasis on meaning and feeling as opposed to form. These ascriptions stand. But the emphasis on meaning does not bring with it any corresponding insistence on clarity. On the contrary, modern dance is wonderful for its obscurity, for its hazily grandiloquent explanations in programme notes of the items on view or, more often than not, for no explanations at all; the action so often seems intended to be symbolic, to carry depths of meaning, but so often no key or not quite the right key is provided. Meaning seems often to be lost in a tangle of feeling; and even that feeling often seems spurious, as though it were less a choreographer's genuine, if muddled, effort to express what he truly felt than a facile 'mish-mash' of portentous movement which he, the choreographer, does not care to explain because any real explanation would show that the Emperor was very scantily clothed, if clothed at all. Yet the odd thing is—and this is the self-contradiction I have in mind—that it is the modernists rather than the classicists who say, and they say it at length and often, that the choreographer's meaning does not matter, that what matters is the quality of the dance itself; and they back this by not so much admitting as insisting on the freedom, sometimes the extreme freedom, of the dancers to construe the choreographer's original intentions according to their own particular fancy. All this, it seems to me, is a hopeless attempt to have it both ways: to pretend to be meaningful and feelingful while, at the same time, brushing aside an accusation of obscurity by asserting that anyhow it is only the movement-quality which counts—and read into it, if you wish, any meaning or none. Let me add at once that I believe this last assertion to be entirely right: that in any dance work, balletic, 'contemporary' or whatever, it is not the meaning (in the sense of a message) but the dance quality which counts. So much so that for the audience, so often fogged by the obscurity, not to say obscurantism of modern dance-works and occasionally by the same vexations in respect of ballet too, a useful rule of thumb is this: do not be bothered by obscurity; do not believe that if a work's obscurity prevents your enjoying it, it is you who are at fault. If the movement-quality is good enough the obscurity, if obscurity there is, will not be an insuperable obstacle to enjoyment; a nuisance, yes perhaps, but no more than that—and quite likely an interesting titillation. Be assured that if the movement-quality is not, of itself, convincing, then the fault is the choreographer's, not yours. A rule of thumb is not infallible; and this one, which takes no account of individual aptitude or ineptitude in appreciating movement-quality, will not always work; but it will do so much more often than not. Obscurity, in short, is the refuge—even the hall-mark—of bad modern or 'contemporary' choreography.

About the all importance of movement-quality—that, in the final analysis, the quality of the dance itself is its own message—more in my next chapter. For the moment let it lie. How curious, though, that the modernists rather than classicists should insist on it; for their works, with their smaller, sometimes much smaller, technical resources, tend to be less viable in terms of movement-quality and to have greater need for the support, however misjudged, of literary meanings and messages. The explanation, I think, is that the classicists take the criterion of movement-quality for granted; there is a nakedness, a self-evidence about the movement-quality of their works; they know that, for good or ill, and however much they may strive after dramatic or literary messages, portentous obscurity will never save them from being judged not on 'contents' but on 'form'; and form is, not indeed exclusively but supremely, classicism.

Summary

I sum up the argument of this chapter. The term 'ballet' has become vague and wide; it needs, for clarity, to be narrowed down, exceptions admitted, to the traditional, classical technique of dancing and to the choreography based on that technique. This technique differs from any other western one, and specifically from the modern types, in being harder to acquire, more stylized and, at the same time, more comprehensive and therefore more adaptable. An empty formalism is the characteristic demerit of its choreography when that choreography is bad, whereas the characteristic demerit of modern choreography, when bad, is formless muddle. 'Contemporary' dance is an expression of the modern romantic revolt against classical disciplines; but this romantic impulse has also been taken into the classical tradition. That tradition can, and to an extent does, absorb the modern romantic movement; modern romantic dance cannot absorb classicism and, in so far as it remains outside the classical tradition, is necessarily ephemeral. In all choreography, classical or other, what matters is the movement-quality not the message or literary meaning; movement-quality, in the final analysis, brings its own message.

Postscript, mainly on jazz

In this chapter I have (you might say) 'written down' modern dance in favour of ballet. Yes, but not written it off. However it may develop, there will be need and room for it, not mainly as a thing in itself, not as peer and rival of the classical tradition, but as a stimulant to it, almost as its licensed gadfly. Nor, come to that, do I write off folk and national dancing, which have their own attractions; but even, or perhaps particularly, in their more theatrical forms, they cannot be regarded as rivals of ballet in which, in any case, they have, from time to time, been partly incorporated. A word, though, about jazz dancing, that potent development of American negro folk dance. It is something separate from the modern movement though considerably merged in it. It has affected ballet too and has conspicuously dominated western social dance during most of this century; it can be captivating and certainly has its own distinct techniques. But again, it no more rivals ballet in range, adaptability and technical demands than does (for instance) Spanish dance with its own long tradition and its highly developed but relatively limited capabilities. Personally I tend to find jazz dancing's 'popular' unintellectual, theatrical manifestations, particularly as adapted by the negro choreographer, Alvin Ailey, or by that master of all styles, Jerome Robbins, more attractive than the cerebrations of much Grahamesque and post-Graham choreography. Given a comparable technical limitation I tend to prefer an air of spontaneity, of sensuous enjoyment, even if these qualities are contrived, to intellectual pretentiousness. That by the way.

I have been concerned with modern or 'contemporary' rather than with jazz or any other form of dance because it alone has had pretensions to rival ballet. I have not said that only ballet is capable of producing works of importance and beauty. That, of course, was not my meaning when, near the beginning of this chapter, I professed to attack the cosy notion that what mattered was not technique but only whether the choreography, in whatever technique, was good or bad. My purpose was, and is, to stress that technique matters like anything and that the classical technique is the best we have. That superiority I have certainly not proved—it is, in the strict sense, unprovable—but I have, I hope, suggested how it may be recognized and why it should be accepted. And that is why, in the next chapter, when I shall try to say what dance (western dance) does best, I shall often be using 'ballet' and 'dance' as interchangeable terms. Not to contradict what was said earlier about the need to disentangle ballet's meaning from latter-day accretions to it, but because what modern theatrical dance does best is, on the whole, best done by ballet.

THREE

What ballet does best

Dance without strings

What ballet does best: there are, it seems to me, many ways of approaching this subject. I list some of them. The business of dance is to dance, not to do what the written, spoken or sung word or a picture, moving or motionless, can do better. That is an obvious starting-point, perhaps the most obvious one. A sub-category of this approach would be a flat statement that all theatrical dance, ballet included, is a poor story-teller, an unsubtle dramatic medium; it would be possible to start from there. Or I might hark back to the observation, made at the end of my introductory historical sketch, that ballet has so proliferated, ventured into so many styles and themes during this century that its potentialities and limitations can now be graded as never before. That would be the historical approach. Or, again, there is the fertile rule, as I once heard it enunciated apropos ballet by Lord (Kenneth) Clark, that an art-form, if it would not wither, must always be seeking to expand its frontiers. A nice by-road, this, of the historical approach. Another starting-point could be the proposition that, although the choreography is a very mutable element in a dance-work, changing much more than the relatively immutable music through the years of performance, the dance is, nevertheless, the great preservative. That proposition, true or not so true, could start the examination. Or it would be possible to name the handful of important choreographers, current or recent, and to take the plunge by examining the characteristics of their work, what has and what has not true merit in it. Or finally, another proposition could be stated: that dance and, within the generality of dance, ballet most of all, is the sexiest of the visual arts and that ballets are memorable because of their sexiness or at least their sensuality. Not everyone, I daresay, would agree with that; but it would get the argument going. In fact, I opt not for one of these approaches but for all (except one) of them. In whatever order I may try to take them, they are, all of them, interrelated, though they do not necessarily all lead in the same direction.

So: ballet is bad at story-telling, weak in drama. Why? Because the silent human body, however well trained, is immensely limited as a communicator of exact meanings when compared with the word, written, spoken or even sung. I take this proposition as self-evident. In practice the evidence is constantly with us. In the classics the dance action is recurrently interrupted so that the protagonists can tell each other about themselves and their problems in a sign language which, though highly developed during the past century, can never make more than simple statements. The dance is one thing and the story, as told in this conventional mime, is something else and, of course, very few of us onlookers can hope to get the story's details, however simple, from the sign language unless aided by programme notes. So here, at the heart of the matter, in the famous classics, we have an elementary example: the dancers dance and then stop from time to time to fill in the story. And even if it is true that the stylized mime has a charm of its own, nevertheless it is an emotional and aesthetic let down, a necessary but jarring interruption to the dance. This was one of the characteristics of the 19th century ballet which irritated Fokine to revolt. He revolted in favour not only of stylistic verisimilitude (that is a separate point) but also of continuous, mime-including dance. A right and proper revolt; an attempt by ballet to widen its frontiers. But an obvious illustration of what happens when this revolt is pushed to the point of trying to put fairly complicated stories into dance form is provided, quite extensively, by the works of one of Fokine's eminent Diaghilevian successors, Leonide Massine. The stories become too complicated to be put into silent movement, so that the audience's need for programme notes becomes in, for instance *The Good Humoured Ladies*, greater than ever; no longer are there passages of pure dance —or at least there are fewer of them—to be enjoyed on their own account but mime and dance are unintelligibly amalgamated. Here I am not thinking of difficulties arising from any attempt to put across profundities of psychological or other drama; I am thinking not of anything so abstruse as that but simply of silent movement's difficulty in telling a story of which the 'action' is a bit complicated though the emotional or intellectual contents may be quite superficial. And when it does come to 'real' drama—the deeper intricacies of human motives and relationships—then ballet (dance) is even worse off. The greater the intellectual-psychological requirements the greater the inadequacy of the dance medium to measure up. As it happens ballet's choreographers, though their technical means are the most comprehensive, are not very prone to this sort of over-ambitiousness; it is, much more, a foible of the moderns; of the best as well as the worst of them—of Martha Graham, for instance, in her glosses on Greek mythology. In ballet aspirations to serious drama tend to get modified into melodrama; but that, too, is a confession of the dance medium's limitations. It can well be sensational—that is, achieve a *coup de théâtre*—but cannot state, much less sustain, any very intelligent argument; nor, except very simply, can it delineate character development nor, except, again very simply, analyse thoughts, feelings, motives, behaviour. In short, dance is at a huge disadvantage when its wordlessness tries to do what, self-evidently, words can do better.

Such are the guide-lines. And if, for the moment at least, we do not question their inviolability, what is left for dance? What can it do? It can dance. The only way I know of explaining the particular potency and beauty of ballet is by analogy with lyric poetry, that is with poetry at its most purely poetic. It is, like all analogies, inexact: lyric poetry, since its instrument is the word, is concerned with verbal meanings as dance is not. But words in lyric even more than in any other kind of poetry have a more than literal meaning; their effectiveness is in their music, their other than purely rational evocativeness, their suggestions of truths and images, sounds, fragments and relationships, which are not to be netted in prose statement or argument. The form of words may be strict—what more formal than a sonnet unless it be the ballet dancer's five positions? —but the meaning is all suggestion, allusion and, perhaps, elusiveness. Yet the impact can be very powerful, because (in my philosophy at least) the world on which lyric poetry is a small, infrequent window is one to which our hearts, our minds too aspire. Dance, and ballet particularly, as the finest realization of western dance, is like that. Especially so when it is truest to itself; when, that is, it puts aside the encumbrances of story, drama, verbal meanings, and simply dances. That is not the same as saying 'when it becomes abstract'. To talk of abstract dance is to talk nonsense. Dance is human bodies in movement and nothing could be less abstract than that. Indeed, it could be argued that a ballet becomes least abstract, or at least that the dancers become most personal, when story, drama, impersonation are least emphatically interposed between them and the audience; it is then that they become most themselves.

Let me illustrate this by Frederick Ashton's choreography for Margot Fonteyn, and specifically by *Symphonic Variations*. This ballet, made shortly after the end of the war, when Ashton and Fonteyn were approaching the peaks of their high capacity, is several things. It is the purest of pure examples of latter-day classicism, totally liberated from mime, drama, narrative; it is—and who so blind as to disagree?—one of the most enduringly beautiful ballets in the British or any other repertory; and, though it has no lime-lit star and though in Fonteyn's autumnal years she has yielded her part in it to younger dancers, it is, of all Ashton's ballets in which she has had a role, the one which most truly and affectionately expresses her. It is much too good a ballet to be allowed to die because she is no longer up to it yet it belongs to her for ever; her successors only have it on loan. And *Symphonic Variations* is about everything and nothing; no story, no drama, not even any *pas de deux*, in any real sense of the term, to suggest an amorous relationship between any of the three girls and three young men who make up its cast; it is just classical dancing set to splendid music, and its ebb and flow of movement, its stillnesses, its weaving and unweaving of human, physical patterns set the imagination roaming. It is like lyric poetry and it is the lyric poetry of dance. When people are not convinced, but are willing to be, that dance (ballet) is a worthwhile art, this is one of the very few specimens to which I refer them. *Symphonic Variations* is ballet's purest essence. That is what it is about.

Another example, from the works of Jerome Robbins, the only choreographer who has given me pleasure comparable with that given by Ashton: his *Dances at a Gathering*. I cannot say whether or not it is as great as, or perhaps even greater than, *Symphonic*, but it is essentially of the same supremely poetic kind—all evocation, all or almost all classical. But there is a difference; for this time there are hints—no more than hints—of other than purely dance-relationships; in this or that of the various *pas de deux* and assorted ensembles which Robbins has put to Chopin's music, there is the

suggestion of the girl left out, of the quaintly aggressive, compet-
itive young man, and so on; there is humour and overall there
is just a whiff of a pervading theme—what is it? Love of the
good earth? Love, more specifically, of Chopin's good Polish earth?
Or simply the joy of dancers in their dancing? The title might
seem to suggest the last of these; and Robbins himself has told us,
'There are no stories to any of the dances ... There are no plots and
no roles. The dancers are themselves dancing with each other to that
music in that space.' There it is: the truth from the choreographer
himself. But is it quite the whole truth? Either way, it does not
matter a bit. What matters is that *Dances* is very beautiful and all of
a piece and that it both satisfies and liberates the imagination. I have
said that *Symphonic Variations* belongs to Fonteyn, that it is somehow 'about' her; the extraordinary thing about Robbins's masterpiece is that, though the Royal Ballet only got it second-hand—it had
been made originally for the New York City company—and though
its performances over here have contained considerable variations
of cast, it always seems to be 'about' the dancers concerned. It is
choreography on which the performers always imprint their personalities. I mean not that, whatever the cast changes, it is always
done equally well, but that, whoever dances it, he or she always
gives us a self-portrait, with an immediacy not to be found in any
dramatic or narrative ballet that I can think of. All this in a ballet
which Covent Garden only got second-hand. I did happen to see
Dances on its very first, its pre-first night performance, by the
NYCB at the Lincoln Centre in 1969 when it certainly made a
strong impression on me, though nothing like so strong as when it
came to Covent Garden and the Royal Ballet. But, from all accounts,
it has provided at least as much self-portraiture of its American
dancers, as might be expected since it was first made on and for
them. I used to think that adaptability to many different, yet valid,
interpretations was one of the chief criteria of supremely good
choreography; it is a test passed superabundantly by *Dances*; passed
also by *Symphonic Variations* though, bearing in mind what I have
said about Fonteyn's ownership, less completely. There are degrees
of ownership, just as there are degrees of choreographic excellence.
Symphonic Variations without the Fonteyn of 15 or more years ago
is *Symphonic Variations* deprived, but still highly admirable,
whereas *The Dying Swan* without Pavlova is dead. Another reminder, this, that general propositions about an art-form, indispensable if sense is to be made of the subject, are never a perfect fit.

Or, again, there is the prodigious Balanchine, the idol among our modern classical choreographers, whose output has been so enormous and who, with his *Agon* and subsequent, similar works, is regarded as having taken pure classicism over a new threshold, to a domain where it can be partnered by the most ascetic, difficult music and, where, if we are persuaded by the panegyrists, the Balanchinesque postures, movements and groupings, strained and contorted as they might sometimes seem to be, are those not of frail human dancers but of Olympians. He might seem paradoxical; on the one hand, his choreography is most impersonal, requiring stringently that his dancers should not express their own personalities at all but should be his passive instruments, while, on the other hand, there is no other choreographer who so insists on a certain kind of (female) dancer; there is a 'Balanchine-type' as there is not a Robbins or Ashton type. But, of course, here is no real incompatibility; on the contrary, it is just because he looks for a type— long limbed, lithe, cool—that he eschews personality. *Agon*, by the way, is Greek for 'struggle' or 'contest', but Balanchine himself has said of this ballet: 'it is less a struggle or contest than a measured construction in space, demonstrated by moving bodies set to certain patterns or sequences in rhythm and melody.' In other words; out with personality and in with cyphers. That, I think, is why I am no Balanchine idolator; to insist on discarding personality rather than to delight, as Ashton and Robbins do, in exploiting and developing it seems to me to rob ballet of one of its greatest enchantments. But this, I add at once, amounts to saying that in choreography, as in everything, seldom is there gain without loss. The corollary to Ashton's delicacy of classicism, his musical sensitivity and his eye for personality is his avoidance of awkward, off-beat subjects. Robbins, so adroit, so poetic, so versatile, is accused by some—is sometimes guilty of—slickness, meretriciousness. And the gain which Balanchine has made is in adding a new, spare, wholly unsentimental poetry to the library of classical dance. He has been an innovator as Ashton and Robbins have not been. (Nor happily, despite what he says, has he quite succeeded in eliminating personality. The human body, Suzanne Farrell's like others, refuses to be impersonal.) We may think of the Ashton of *Symphonic Variations* as the most traditional of the three, the Robbins of *Dances* as the most 'popular', the nearest to everyman's taste, and the Balanchine of *Agon* as the boldest, the most original. But what they have in common is that they have made ballets in the classical tradition, each in (thank goodness) his own way, which are analogous to lyric poetry and express ballet's essence.

Adventures in trespass

Is that, you may well ask, the whole of it? Granted that this kind is ballet at its purest, should nothing else be attempted? What about the proposition that an art-form should always be striving to extend its frontiers? Is not this kind of ballet a retreat into an ivory tower rather than an attempt at expansion? As to this last question, while I am sure that the Clark dictum about frontier extension is useful I am not convinced at all that it provides the only criterion of an art's vitality. It needs qualification, elaboration. For instance, *Symphonic Variations*, *Dances at a Gathering* and *Agon*, even *Agon*, may not be classifiable as extensions of ballet's frontiers, but they are a development of what was best in Petipa; a throw-back, if you like, across the more obviously romantic, expansionist years of Diaghilev to the original source, to the basic strength on which all ballet depends. Not in order to make pastiche of Petipa's *Bayadère* or *Rose Adagio* or Ivanov's white act of *Swan Lake*, but to enrich the Petipa–Ivanov tradition by intensifying its poetic potency; in short, a very real development and beautiful evidence not of atrophy but of life. So, again, while indicating that complications of narrative may easily become too much for silent movement to manage, I have also indicated that there are simplicities of narrative and characterization which lie within the 'natural' scope of ballet—interpretable by expressive or mimed dance. Such narrative ballets are probably not to be regarded as extensions of the frontiers. Yet they represent a real achievement, of a sort unknown before Fokine and greatly developed since his time. To say that is to recognize that there is, of course, no fixed point at which narrative and characterization become too complicated, abstruse and profound to be contained 'naturally' in ballet; the frontiers are not a barbed wire fence. Nevertheless, the question remains: is ballet's every development, other than pure dance and the simple narrative which is close kin to pure dance, a misdirection of effort? So: back to the guide-lines. Are they, in fact, inviolable?

They are not. I drew them peremptorily because it is important to realize what comes most readily to dance and what strains it, where it is most at home and where least. They were meant as a warning, not as an absolute deterrent (as the former they may be some use; if meant as the latter they have clearly been no use at all). Not prohibitive rules but signposts intended to show where so many ballets and, more generally, dance-works go wrong. Not, however, intended to damn all such past adventures or to stop the adventurers from trying again. But because ballet (dance) nowadays is so prone to adventure and because, in this century, there have been so many misadventures, so these guide-lines are now particularly necessary. And, with so much evidence available, they now (I repeat) have a chance, as never before, of being enduringly serviceable.

It might now be useful to look at some successful specimens of other than pure dance-works, in order to discover what, if any, common denominator there is to the reasons for their success. They have included narrative dance-works in many technical idioms, ranging from the almost unadulterated classical through the classical-modern to the wholly modern; there have been tragedies, comedies, psychological dramas, melodramas, semblances of ritual, works fraught with messages, erotic works. In almost every western dance idiom or blend of idioms, used for almost every imaginable subject, there have been successes as well as a huge dump-heap of failures. So I shall now list some successes of the Diaghilevian period and since. Some seem to me significant because they exemplify what can be done within the (admittedly inexact) frontiers of dance's fairly evident capacity; but there are others, the adventures across those frontiers, and to them should be given the special attention which I think they deserve.

ASHTON's *Fille mal gardée*: a simple narrative comedy in which, throughout the three scenes, the dance, story, mime and form are all joined in a sustained flow of almost wholly classical inventiveness. Also Ashton's *The Dream*, a wonderfully adroit adaptation of *A Midsummer's Night's Dream* to terms of classical dance and silent comedy.

ANTONY TUDOR's *Echoing of Trumpets, Shadowplay, Lilac Garden, Pillar of Fire* and *Dark Elegies*: all of them intensely dramatic; all, except perhaps *Dark Elegies*, based, closely for the most part, on classicism; all uniting, inseparably, the action with the dance.

ROBBINS's *The Cage*: female spiders and their doomed mates; dramatic, cruel, relentless; done in a mixture of predominant classicism with many modernist touches. *Fancy Free*: American sailors on shore-leave; a marvel of fun and inventiveness in its time (1944); jazz-classical mixture, a bit dated now. Also his *Afternoon of a Faun* (classicism, ballet dancers' narcissism, academic exercises-cum-sensuality) and *Les Noces*, a stylistic blend of the classical and the modern to ritualistic effect. Both of these are impertinently happy remakes, the one of Nijinsky's obsolete, once sensational *Faun*, the other of Nijinska's beautiful, far from obsolete *Les Noces*.

NIJINSKA's original *Les Noces*: even better than Robbins's remake; simple, only faintly classical, ritualistic, tremendous.

BALANCHINE's *Ivesiana*: thoroughly unclassical, creepy-crawly and, so far as I remember it, highly effective. Also his *Bugaku*, an erotic adaptation from Japanese ritual to western neo-classicism; horrifying (I believe) to the Japanese, 'but oh! delighting me'. Also *Cotillon*, a lovely, lost early (1932) Balanchine ballet which perhaps should not be put on this list because its off-classical character sketches might almost as well put it in the category of the pure dancing *Symphonic Variations* and *Dances at a Gathering*. A borderline case (and only distantly remembered). And two-thirds of *The Prodigal Son*: imaginative stylization of the biblical story (the ending, however, is stylistically and dramatically weak).

ANDRÉE HOWARD's *La Fête Etrange*: an off-classical evocation of the central episode of Alain-Fournier's *Le Grand Meaulnes*; dance and mime blended. Close to the borderline, not because of any doubt about its quality but because it is so near to being dance's pure lyric poetry.

AGNES DE MILLE's *Fall River Legend*: a psychological murder story; strong, simple movements, dramatic, potent. Also her *Rodeo*: folk-dance made theatrical, and a simple, danceable theme.

KENNETH MACMILLAN's *The Invitation*: a largely classical-style drama about adolescent sex; again dance and action well blended. And the less thoroughly successful *Hermanas*, a Lorca play turned into off-classical movement. Also his version of *The Rite of Spring*, strong, unclassically stylized, ritualistic, and his *Romeo and Juliet*, which is carried spendidly by its several big moments of lyrical, off-classical dance; it is the crowd scenes which need the carrying.

JOHN CRANKO's *Eugene Onegin*: a clever, three-act adaptation of opera to ballet, with some fine *pas de deux* and solos (classical) as its highlights. Also his *Taming of the Shrew*; it flags towards the end, but (most rare) is very funny; and essentially classical. His

Romeo and Juliet might just be included—much weaker than Mac-Millan's in the climactic lyrical episodes but much more effective in its crowd scenes.

LEONIDE MASSINE's *Le Beau Danube*: which, when done as it once was and never is nowadays, is an almost perfect little specimen of off-classical style-cum-simple story. Also his *Three Cornered Hat* which, though it is burdened with too intricate a story for its dance to manage, used to be gloriously redeemed by Massine's own dancing. Alas, it has no such redemption nowadays. Like *Beau Danube* and unlike *Cotillon* it still gets performed; but it is, I fear, a wraith nowadays if not quite a lost work.

HANS VAN MANEN's *Twilight*: only a *pas de deux* but memorably effective in its erotic, part-classical, part-modern, gimmicky way (the gimmick is the girl's dancing in high-heeled shoes which, in the latter part of the *pas de deux*, she then discards).

MARTHA GRAHAM's *Primitive Mysteries* and *El Penitente*: these are far from being Graham's only successes but they are the best examples I know of her (for me) greatest choreographic achievement: the use of a stylization of her own to produce an extraordinarily strong sense of ritual—simple, moving, dramatic.

This list may seem idiosyncratic. It might seem less so, or possibly more, were I listing only my favourites. At any rate, some of the works mentioned would then be excluded and others, in the pure dance category, would come in; for instance, Fokine's *Sylphides*, Balanchine's *Serenade, Liebeslieder Waltzer*, and perhaps his *Episodes* and *Apollo*; Glen Tetley's *Voluntaries*, and others besides. My present purpose, however, is not that but to give examples of what, in other than a pure dance idiom, seem to be significant successes; and (I re-emphasize it) especially of those works which, according to the guide-lines I drew, can be categorized as successfully adventurous trespasses beyond the frontiers.

Stylization

Various points arise. The first is that I hope readers will have seen, or will see, enough of the works listed to judge from their own experience the sense or nonsense of my judgements. Whether or not that is a reasonable hope I shall have failed unless my generalizations are persuasive enough to act as a guide to determining whether and why a given dance-work has been successful, no matter whether that work is on my list or not. Other points which arise are: drama, ritual, narrative, eroticism—and Antony Tudor. And all these reduce to one point: stylization.

Stylization is not quite all; but it is a great deal. In some of the examples I have given it does not obtrude as a problem solved. That is because these—Ashton's *Dream* and *Fille mal gardée*, Andrée Howard's *Fête Etrange*, and others—are more or less comfortably within the narrative or dramatic capacity of the classical idiom. These are the untroublesome specimens; I put them on the list only as a reminder of how successful a narrative or dramatic ballet can be, provided the story is simple enough and/or the choreography is dominated by lyrical quality, rather than by an attempt to convey difficult or complicated, word-requiring meanings. That, indeed, is not to denigrate Ashton's *Fille* (a seemingly endless profusion of happy inventiveness, a choreographic counterpart, I dare to say, to the melodic richness and felicity of Schubert's *Great C Major Symphony*) or his *Dream* (which so artfully makes choreographic coherence of *A Midsummer's Night's Dream*, avoiding over-complication and making the ballet not just a commentary on Shakespeare but a beautiful thing in itself), or Andrée Howard's *Fête Etrange* (again, an adaptation from literature, and so delicately done that, as I said earlier, it is almost on the borderline between pure lyricism and narrative). But these, as I say, are the beautifully easy ones; significant not because they extend frontiers (they do not) but because they so well illustrate what comes 'naturally' to ballet.

In Massine's *Three Cornered Hat* the question of stylization does obtrude; this is, after all, the one and only example I know of Spanish style used to make a successful ballet—and used by a Russian at that, not by a Spaniard. But, whether he used it well or ill, the choice of style was no problem; given the story, the setting and, especially, the music, it just had to be Spanish. I have put it on my list not only, nor mainly, as an example of stylization but because it is, in another sense, an exception: a ballet which does not succeed in making its story wholly intelligible in terms of dance—it has too many minor complications, explicable only by a programme note—but which has succeeded, all the same, under particular circumstances; that is when it has the right dancer for its main role. The fact that this has not happened since Massine himself became too old for it makes me think that it is unlikely to happen again. Another reminder, this, of the frailty of generalizations: there is a basic weakness in *The Three Cornered Hat* yet who cared about that when Massine danced it? Or who cares about the tedium of the crowd scenes in Kenneth MacMillan's version of *Romeo and Juliet* when it comes to the gorgeous sequences of expressive, passionate dance by Juliet and her Romeo in the balcony and bedroom scenes and, not quite as potently, in the Capulets' ballroom?

The point, however, is obvious and I have perhaps laboured it: that certain dance-works, however defective, can and at times do succeed for a variety of reasons: because they are 'vehicles' for a particular star, because they contain a memorable choreographic movement or two, compensating for the forgettable remainder, because—well, the reasons are endless. But exceptions are poor guides. And stylization is the key if we would understand why and how dance can and does extend its frontiers.

I have mentioned ritual. All dance is, in a sense, ritualistic, in that it formalizes, or should formalize, movement. But that sense is too indeterminate to be useful here. What I have in mind is the kind of dance-work which, more specifically, puts across a ceremony, a rite, in such a way as to give it validity as a staged spectacle. This means something other than merely transferring a religious or other ceremony to the stage; it entails, at the least, a very positive adaptation. Sometimes the real life ritual may be quite close to its stage stylization—an example, I think, is Martha Graham's *El Penitente* —or sometimes it may be only a suggestion which on stage becomes enriched—such is the Russian peasant wedding as transmuted by Nijinska into *Les Noces*—or sometimes the ceremony may be wholly imaginary, as it is in *The Rite of Spring*, and in Martha Graham's *Primitive Mysteries*. To judge from my examples ballet seems to be, if anything, less proficient than non-balletic techniques as a purveyor of ritual. *Les Noces* is perhaps partly classical, *The Rite of Spring* (MacMillan's version) is not at all, though both of them do certainly require to be danced by the classically trained. No modern dancer whom I have seen could cope, as Monica Mason does for the Royal Ballet, with MacMillan's solo for the Chosen Maiden, or for that matter, with Nijinska's solo in *Les Noces* for bridesmaid and best man. Perhaps this is the answer: that ballet's technique, unadulterated, makes for so distinctive a stylization that it is hard to accept it as a ritual adapted from any other source—as, within limits, a dramatic language, yes, but not quite as a religious or other ritual. I do not, however, know.

What I feel much surer about is that, in my time, Martha Graham has been the greatest ritualist of them all. My list included her *El Penitente* and *Primitive Mysteries*, of which the latter is particularly remarkable; it is a deeply moving, and in no way offensive evocation of the Crucifixion as seen through Mary's eyes; simple and beautiful, a silent mystery play to end all mystery plays. How on earth does she do it? I think the weightiness—the 'gravitas', rather —of the Graham technique has something to do with it; but I also think that in whatever idiom she happened to work she would have the sense of it: the sense, that is, of the emotional force which prompts religious feeling and, accordingly, of the way to express that feeling. This sense pervades her works; it is a large part of their distinctive strength. So much so that I, with my very evident preference, or prejudice, for ballet, sometimes think that when this great modern choreographer rejected classicism and went her own way, an even greater choreographer was still-born. Martha Graham equipped with the classical technique—what might she not have given us! But then that Martha would have been different in other ways as well. Idle speculations... Can staged ritual be regarded as an extension of dance's frontiers? Surely it can; and it is a development which has occurred not often but notably in western dance during this century. Religious practice is not the only source of ritual: but it is one big source. It is perhaps odd to reflect that our latter-day choreographers, not religiously motivated at all (not even 'the high priestess of modern dance', as Martha Graham has been called, is prompted by religious motives), should have re-established a link between religious ritual and dance. In some other civilizations this link has never been broken. Think of the rigmarole of Hindu mythology which is part and parcel of Indian dance; think of 'Hindu temple dancers'—the term speaks for itself. But in western civilization the link has persisted only in the backwoods; among the Mexican peasants, for instance, from whom Martha Graham culled *El Penitente*. Yes, surely a rediscovery which amounts to a new development.

Balanchine's *Bugaku* might well have been included among my examples of ritual. Ritualistic it is; more precisely, it is an essentially classical ballet inspired by a Japanese marital ritual and, to the Japanese mind, so brazenly transmuted from Oriental reticence to occidental explicitness that good Japanese manners will have none of it. It is the most erotic dance-work I know. That is, unless this titillating description should be shared with Hans van Manen's duet called *Twilight* or, for that matter, with *Dances at a Gathering* or

La Fille mal gardée or even *Swan Lake*. I am not just joking. All dance is more or less sensual; it cannot but be since it is about human bodies and, very very often, about male and female in partnership. The highly stylized dance which we know as ballet may rarefy this sensuality. But that is also a way of saying that such highly stylized choreography can do much which, if presented realistically, would be gross. Nowadays almost anything goes; almost realistic sex has become a theatrical commonplace, in dance—some modern dance—along with the rest. But that, paradoxically or not, is far from meaning that the more realistic the realism the more erotic the effect. In fact, stark realism breeds quick disenchantment. I think this has always been so, not only when realism is two a penny, as it is now. In these matters imagination is (almost) all; and, in dance, imagination's prompter is stylization. These, however, are matters of highly individual taste; and while I would not contend that *Swan Lake* is, for me, the most erotic of dance-works, I would not be much surprised if some people found it so. After all, if cultivated Japanese are repelled rather than exhilarated by what they regard as the vulgar frankness of *Bugaku*, there may well be perfectly reasonable occidentals—there are; I have met them—to whom a polite Japanese level of stylization might, indeed, seem unexcitingly reticent but who would find the—how shall I put it?—elegant legginess of *Swan Lake* as erotic as anything. For some people the whole attraction of ballet, and part of its attraction for almost everyone, is that it is a leg-show with the label 'art' attached to it. More than that, it is a particularly good, suggestive, stimulating, disturbing (you have a choice of adjectives) leg-show just because it not only wears but deserves its 'art' label.

Lord (Kenneth) Clark, in his classic *The Nude*, remarked that good art could carry a lot of sex; not only is the corollary true—that sex can carry a lot of art—but if sex does so then it will seem all the sexier to the very many whose taste is at least slightly imaginative rather than utterly gross. So, what I do contend is that somewhere along the dance spectrum between the opposite extremes of almost stark realism and almost totally reticent stylization there is a point where stylization and explicitness fuse into the maximum eroticism. That point will be a bit different for almost everybody; the amount of stylization which will mark it will vary according to taste but for many, even for the majority of tastes, it will be quite a long way along the spectrum towards stylization's extreme. I have said that for me, personally, *Bugaku* and, I add, van Manen's little *Twilight* are just about at that point. It seems to me that ballet in our time, sometimes with an admixture of modern style (*Twilight*), sometimes without it (*Bugaku*), has much developed the erotic element latent in dance stylization. Does this qualify as a genuine development or as a debasement? As the former, surely.

Drama

I have left dance drama till last. It is the largest category, also the most awkward one because it is particularly fraught with question-marks about the capacity of the language of dance, about its disadvantage when it challenges, or seems to challenge, comparison with the spoken word. Large as this category is, I might have made it larger still; the three types of dance-work which I have separated from it—the ritualistic, the erotic and the simple, readily danceable narrative ballets—are, all of them, more or less dramatic; there is a kind of drama in ritual, the erotic may well be dramatic and, for that matter, pure dance, which is not so much a category as the golden thread which binds them all, contains a kind of drama. That these distinctions are arbitrary I would not allow; but I would agree at once that their edges are blurred. Of course they are. Of course, compartmentalization, in considering any art, cannot be absolute, as I have said before. But, as I have also said, it is the only way of making sense of the subject. And when I now bring up dramatic ballets as a category I am thinking of those specimens included in my list, and of others like them, which seem to me to have stretched the capacity of silent movement by doing successfully what, on the face of it, could be better done by words. Works which seem successfully to have defied the guide-lines. But that is the nub of the matter; they have not really defied the guide-lines at all; they have circumvented them. They have succeeded because their choreographers, by instinct or awareness, have appreciated, and have had the skill to apply their appreciation, that dance can never—but never —successfully ape the spoken word, with all its width of range and its subtleties of detail, but can sometimes provide a broader, less exact but effective alternative, one which suggests rather than states, which stirs the imagination rather than answers questions, which operates within careful boundaries rather than ranges freely and which, in sum, is stylization.

Balanchine, Robbins, Fokine, Massine, Cranko, MacMillan, Graham, even Ashton—all the notable choreographers of our times have been, to some extent, dramatists. For instance, Robbins's spidery *Cage* is a truly sinister drama, mostly classical in idiom. And MacMillan's *Invitation*, again dominantly classical, is most apt in its simple characterization and very well constructed towards and around its climax (a rape, by the way—what might easily have been only melodramatic is touched wih tragic poignancy).

Among these dramatists, however, there is one who is not occasional; he is Antony Tudor, a dramatist all the time and, in the present context, the most relevant choreographer of them all. Hence the large number of his works on my list. He has been called ballet's first psychological dramatist; often, after witnessing the efforts of his emulators, I have felt that he was the last of them as well. The first time he did the trick was in *Lilac Garden* at the Ballet Rambert's tiny Mercury Theatre in 1936: the trick of impregnating classical movement with hints of character, relationships, reservations, desires, a whole medicine cabinet of human motivations. He has been doing it, with variations, ever since. I suppose that *Pillar of Fire* and *Lilac Garden* are his most typical achievements, both being explorations of the heart, a woman's heart in each instance. But the variations are just as significant: *Echoing of Trumpets*, which is just about the only dance-work in my experience to deal successfully with the horrors of war and contemporary tyranny, subjects so often treated with loud inadequacy by the modernists; *Dark Elegies*, which is a lament for dead children; and *Shadowplay*, which is in an elusive, allusive class all of its own—what exactly is it? Clearly it was prompted, however distantly, by Kipling's *Jungle Book* or at least by Koechlin's Kipling-prompted music; and from that suggestion Tudor has sketched a silent drama about the state of man, as distinct from the state of animals. Or that, at least, is what I think it is about though others, with Tudor's inscrutable blessing, are entirely free to think otherwise. The constant in Tudor is a basically classical or, more often, conspicuously classical technique—least conspicuous perhaps in *Dark Elegies* but basic there too; that and the use of this technique to carry meanings, or half meanings, evocations and implications far deeper and more abstruse than are ordinarily and superficially associated with arabesque, pirouette or *développé*. An achievement, indeed.

Sometimes, even frequently, the Tudor trick does not work. Little wonder, seeing how difficult it is. When it does succeed it is a triumph of stylization, a convincing adaptation of (almost) intractable material into the terms of mostly classical movement. When it fails it is because, in one of two ways, the stylization has broken down. By the sort of irony which besets artistic creativeness, it happens that Tudor is a poor craftsman. Not from him the easy, Ashtonesque flow of inventiveness, made possible by an immediate command of the full wealth of the classical vocabulary; instead there is hard, painful slogging, today's few steps laboriously rehearsed only to be discarded tomorrow. With Ashton the dancers often have the impression that they are really the choreographers, because he has a way of encouraging them to invent this and that and then moulding their sketches to his own choreographic plan; he uses his instrument so adroitly that the instrument often has the illusion of being the master. Not so with Tudor; no dancer in a Tudor ballet ever had the illusion that he or she made it up; there is, on the contrary, a thorough awareness of trying and trying again to find that one expressive movement or position for which the choreographer himself is also groping, with a command of the 'language' which seems less than absolute and is certainly not at his fingertips.

One explanation of Tudor's relative laboriousness might be that he came late (in fact, when he was grown-up) to ballet; but, then, so did Ashton. Another, less assailable explanation is, of course, that Tudor is after a more elusive quarry; that, hard as it is to match music with 'pure dance' which is not just a poor relation but a beautiful thing in itself, it is even harder to give more than superficially dramatic, more than merely melodramatic, expressiveness to classical movement. But that, too, does not quite explain the apparent limitations of Tudor's choreographic vocabulary. At any rate in his works the stylization from time to time breaks down, either by wilting (still a stylization but an inexpressive one) or, more often, by lapsing entirely into barren realism. Examples of the former are in the repetitions of posture and movement in *Lilac Garden* and, of the latter, in the (literally) monkey business of the Terrestrials in *Shadowplay*. Those are examples taken from memorable overall successes. Much less successful, to my mind, is the Tudor version of *Romeo and Juliet* (set to Delius not Prokofiev) because here the choreographer, having had the charming idea of telling the story as though it were a series of Renaissance frescoes, has quite failed to sustain his initial Veronese (or Florentine or Sienese) style; realism supervenes, stylistic and, therefore, dramatic unity is dissipated and the result is a might-have-been, a promise unfulfilled; the idea was very Tudor and its semi-demi-fulfilment is also characteristic of this errant, adventurous genius's tendency to bite off more than he can chew. Tudor, in his failures as in his successes, is a text to preach from. No one else has done so much to make ballet's stylizations take in worthwhile drama; no one else has shown how tough a task this is.

He or, more specifically, his *Shadowplay* serves as text for another lesson too. *Shadowplay* is an obscure ballet, or so I have said. I have interpreted it to my own, though I daresay, not to others' satisfaction, and Tudor, the ever enigmatic, will not tell us what he meant it to mean. It is right to suspect that the reason for not explaining obscure choreography is either that the meaning would turn out to be trivial or that a gap would be shown between the choreographer's intention and his execution. But in this instance, I suspect, the suspicion would be misdirected. Here is no bad choreographer taking refuge in obscurity but a very fine, if uneven, one telling us, in effect, to judge his work on its movement-quality. And, he might add, if we find the movements not only beautiful but variously evocative, so much the better; for that power of evocation, that poetic power, is a property of the best choreography. Well, it is not only good choreographers who ask to be judged in terms of movement-quality; the bad ones do it too. But only the good ones, like Tudor, come through that definitive judgement unscathed.

So I return to the question with which this chapter began; what does ballet (dance) do best? In trying to answer it I have laid down guide-lines, not to set inviolable limits but to indicate what comes most naturally to this art of silent movement—that is, without strain to its capacity—and what takes it, perilously, over its natural, though not exactly definable frontiers into the territory of the spoken word. I have noted various categories in which, as it seems to me, the achievements (and failures) of ballet (dance) in our time can be placed: the 'pure dance', the relatively simple narrative, the ritualistic, the erotic and—large pantechnicon—the dramatic. In the course of doing this I have mentioned but perhaps not sufficiently insisted that 'pure dance', though distinguishable, is not really a category like the rest. I insist now: pure dance, being the essence of ballet, can be not only the sum total, the whole purpose of certain works but is also the element which infuses all successful ballets, belonging to whatever category; it is really a synonym for movement-quality, and a synonym again for effective stylization. So, eventually, I come to a very simple answer about all these categories of success. It is an answer which was foreshadowed when, in the previous chapter, I said that the audience should not be greatly bothered about a dance-work's meaning, if that meaning is obscure, but should judge it by its movement-quality. This answer was, in effect, given again just now about the dramatic, stylized, obscure and beautiful *Shadowplay*. In the last analysis it is the movement-quality which counts.

All very well, you may say, but can movement-quality really be wholly divorced from the intended meaning? Does it really not matter what the movements express or whether they express any meaning at all? A difficult one to answer, in theory, but, in practice, not too troublesome. No problem arises in the vast majority of cases. In a specimen of pure dance the meaning is no worry; it is not looked for apart from the movements themselves. And in nearly all specimens of other kinds, if they are good, meaning and movement go hand in hand. So, in practice, the problem is limited to those rarities of more or less dramatic choreography which tend very strongly towards pure dance, with all the potency of poetic, variable evocation which that implies. And about this small, cherishable category I maintain that the meaning intended by the choreographer matters only because it has prompted a work of high movement-quality. Yes, the meaning *is* expendable; it is the scaffolding, not the building. None of my categories (I have said it often enough) is absolute; they all have blurred edges. And just as pure dance is not abstract but highly personal and, maybe, sensual and, possibly, dramatic, so there are stylizations of silent drama (*Shadowplay* a shining example) which go beyond literary exactitude to the lyric poetry of pure dance. So, I repeat, it is movement-quality which counts; and though movement-quality is not achieved by the 'hey presto' of stylization, without stylization it cannot be achieved at all. What ballet does best is whatever it manages effectively to stylize. The purest of pure dance ballets and the most dramatic must ultimately pass the same test; that of (synonymously) effective stylization or movement-quality.

FOUR

Why a ballet lasts

Some reasons why

There was an obvious omission from the last chapter. I treated ballet as though choreography were the whole of it; tried to say what ballet did best with scarcely a word about music and design; with almost nothing to suggest that they made a difference to a ballet's or other dance-work's quality. There was another omission. At the start of the chapter I mentioned several possible approaches to the subject—what ballet does best—and among them was the proposition that, if a ballet or other dance-work endured, that should be credited to its choreography. Though it might be much altered during years of performance it was, nevertheless, this mutable choreography, because of some basic quality in its original version, which bestowed longevity. Not, I said, a proposition necessarily to be agreed with, but one of several possible launching-pads for the argument. Unlike the other possible approaches I mentioned, this one (and only this one) I did not use.

These two omissions went together; neither was unwitting. To say that it is choreography which distinguishes ballet (dance) from any other performing art is virtually to utter a tautology. It seemed to me best, for clarity's sake, to begin by isolating this obviously distinctive ingredient for separate analysis. And it would have been impossible to pursue the proposition that ballets live or die according to the worth of their choreography without breaking this isolation, without, that is, bringing in the ancillaries, design (composed of decor and costumes) and music.

Here that isolation ends. It ends with a denial that the proposition I mentioned holds water or, as the Babu said, enough good water. Not that it is entirely wrong; but it is not right enough to serve as a guide-line through what is, again, a quite tangled object. What is meant by the survival of a ballet or other dance-work? Can it be said to survive if one or more of its original ingredients, including the choreography, has altered? Or, if it can be said to retain its identity despite some alterations, after how much alteration is that identity lost? Does an alteration to the designs or music matter as much as one to the choreography? These are the questions, or some of them, implicit in an attempt to answer the prime one: what makes a ballet or other dance-work last? But, having posed these 'supplementaries' let me, again for the sake of clarity, store them away. There they are; whether or not they are neatly answerable, they will have to be taken out of the store-cupboard and looked at in due course; but not just yet.

It is the business of ballet to dance. Yet I believe that—many exceptions admitted—the choreography, that heart of ballet's matter, that ingredient which distinguishes ballet (dance) from any other performing art, is not usually the main preservative. There are long-living ballets which are successes of music or successes of decor and costume much more than of choreography or, for that matter, of performance by the dancers. And if I were to risk any general statements about the reasons for a ballet's longevity, not, this time, to tickle up an argument but because I believed them, they would be:

That no ballet survives only because of its choreography.

That the choreography may, however, be one of several contributors to that survival; so may the scenario.

That a few ballets survive largely, but not solely, because of their designs.

That the most frequent, the strongest reason for a ballet's survival is its music; even when it is not the only, or apparently the main, reason, it is always an indispensable one.

Music

Having stated these propositions I must try to prove them—by illustration, which is I think, the only way they can be proved. First, the music.

There is music intended for dancing and music not so intended; ballet uses both. There is music written for a specific ballet and music not so written; ballet again uses both. Very often previously existing music is arranged, modified and orchestrated for a specific ballet; and that may be dance-music, in the broad sense, or it may be operatic or symphonic or 'chamber' or whatever; ballet uses the lot. There are all these distinctions among the scores used for ballet and their border lines can be very blurred. Stravinsky wrote music specifically for *The Firebird, Petrouchka* and *The Rite of Spring*; he wrote *Agon* for Balanchine's ballet of the same title; he wrote *Apollo* to be danced, and Adolph Bolm, not Balanchine, was its first choreographer, but it is the Balanchine version which survives; for *Cimarosiana* he arranged and re-orchestrated Cimarosa and, similarly, Pergolesi for *Pulcinella*. Rossini did not intend his occasional, drawing-room entertainments to become the music of *Boutique Fantasque*, but Respighi arranged them specifically for that ballet, as Tommasini did Scarlatti's harpsichord solos for *The Good Humoured Ladies*. Verdi might have been horrified to find his arias and choruses become the accompaniment to *The Lady and the Fool* but the Verdi selection so used was made specifically for that ballet. And so on. The variety of music used for ballet seems to cover the whole spectrum, from Beethoven's *Grosse Fuge* to Minkus, or from Brahms's Fourth Symphony—appropriated, unaltered, for Massine's choreography—to Stravinsky's *Petrouchka*, composed in the closest possible collaboration with Diaghilev, Fokine and Benois. All this bears on music's contribution to a ballet's longevity and I shall try to say how.

The handy test

For some of the music used for ballet there is a handy test; one which applies, pre-eminently, to music composed for a specific ballet, rather more loosely, though I think usefully, to previously existing music which has been adapted for a ballet—and not at all to the 'absolute', self-sufficient music which ballet, nowadays, often takes over, undoctored, unarranged. The test is that if the music lives on independently in the concert hall, then you can (almost) count upon it: sooner or later, and frequently rather than seldom, there will be a revival of the ballet which is attached to that music. A few of this century's examples: de Falla's *Three Cornered Hat*, Ravel's *Daphnis and Chloe*, Poulenc's *Les Biches*, Prokofiev's *Romeo and*

Juliet and, to a lesser extent, his *Cinderella*, Stravinsky's *Rite of Spring, Petroushka, Firebird* and almost any other ballet music by this composer you care to think of. These scores persist independently and they are, all of them, a big reason, if not necessarily the only one, why the ballets attached to them recur on stage.

A handy test I call it. I hope it is that. I do not pretend that it is infallible, far from it, because the distinction between independently surviving concert music and music excluded from that exalted category cannot be hard and fast, particularly in these days when so much music of every conceivable sort is heard ('independently') on the radio. Nevertheless, it provides, I suggest, a useful guide-line. And having applied it to a few, conspicuous examples of the 20th century, let me now see how it works with the survivors from the 19th.

Even nowadays when there are so many ballet companies, and so many of them on the hunt for something, anything, unfamiliar to touch up their hackneyed repertories, only a handful of 19th century works survive; and of those, *Giselle, La Sylphide*, the old warhorse *Don Quixote* and the one act of *La Bayadère* which remains to us, both at Covent Garden and elsewhere, represent a considerable proportion. Their scores, in common with all the music used by 19th century ballet, were specially composed for them. But Adam's score for *Giselle* scarcely qualifies as a concert item: still less does the Hermann von Lovenskjold for *La Sylphide* or the Minkus for *Don Quixote* and *La Bayadère*. So these ballets are eligible for my handy test and, with the semi-demi-exception of *Giselle*, they fail it: the music is not the main reason why they survive. They are, if not quite exceptions, then 'minority cases'; and about them more later. On the other hand, none of them, apart from *Giselle*, begins to compare with the Tchaikovsky–Petipa–Ivanov classics, *Swan Lake, The Sleeping Beauty* and *The Nutcracker* in persistent, unquestionable popularity. Tchaikovsky's music for those three ballets certainly passes the test: it lives on independently and is, overwhelmingly, the main reason why these ballets survive inexhaustibly on stage. If eyebrows rise at that assertion I shall be surprised. Surely no one believes that the vitality of these classics owes anything like as much to Petipa and Ivanov as it does to Tchaikovsky. Pseudo-purism dies hard, I know; new versions—numerous—of *Beauty* and—countless—of *Swan Lake* always carry the emblem of 'choreography after Petipa' (*Beauty*) and 'after Ivanov and Petipa' (*Swan Lake*), but they are riddled with admitted interpolations by later choreographers, and we are certain of the authenticity of nothing beyond Ivanov's Act II of *Swan Lake* and Petipa's *Rose Adagio* and, perhaps, the final *pas de deux* of *The Sleeping Beauty*. The *Nutcracker* has, of course, been abandoned by the purists, except for a finger hold on the leaky raft of the (alleged) Ivanov *grand pas de deux*. What we can be much more certain about is Tchaikovsky's contribution which, despite the tinkering of Minkus, Drigo and Pugni, survives in authentic abundance—or rather in superabundance, for it is constantly amended for the stage by the removal of this or that item and the insertion of another, whether from the 1876 version or from elsewhere along the trail of Tchaikovsky's music for dance; but however amended and re-jigged, it is always there, an apparently irresistible invitation to decade after decade of producers and choreographers to present these ballets again and yet again. Delibes's *Coppelia*, by the way, is comparable; so is his *Sylvia*—not, admittedly, revived anything like so often but, whenever it is revived, owing nothing to its original choreography (is there any record of it or, for that matter, of that of *Coppelia*?) and everything to its familiar and always popular music.

What applies to music written for a specific ballet applies also, though less neatly, to ballet scores arranged from previously existing music. Most, but not all, such scores are taken from music which, before being so arranged, was anyway written for dance or at least was eminently danceable. Many of these arranged scores live on independently; and they pass my handy test—the ballets for which they were arranged are almost certain of at least intermittent revival. But some do not pass. For instance, the Respighi–Rossini for *La Boutique Fantasque* is a concert piece whereas the Tommasini–Scarlatti for *The Good Humoured Ladies* is not, or is much less so, though it too is quite danceable. The Scarlatti, undoctored, unarranged, lives on in concerts, but not the Tommasini–Scarlatti. And if, unlike *La Boutique Fantasque*, *The Good Humoured Ladies* is scarcely revivable (as its revival by the Royal Ballet only served to show), that is partly because of the undanceable complications of its plot, about which I have already said a word, but partly too because the Tommasini–Scarlatti is not tempting enough; were it more tempting the ballet would get on stage, much helped, incidentally, by Bakst's *ottocento* designs—and never mind the plot's complications.

I spoke just now of 'eminently danceable' music. It is a phrase on which I must linger a moment, for it covers many variations. It covers, obviously, music written to be danced, or at least in dance rhythms, though dancers may sometimes be aghast at what they are expected to cope with even in music written for a specific ballet (the rhythmic intricacies, for instance, of Stravinsky's *Rite of Spring*). But it does not necessarily exclude music which originally was vocal, even operatic, or instrumental music of all sorts. A list of successful musical arrangements for ballet (excluding original compositions for a specific work) might show a predominance of, broadly speaking, dance music—a predominance but no monopoly. The score made for Massine's *Mam'zelle Angot* out of Lecocq's operetta *La Fille de Mme Angot* and Charles Mackerras's arrangement for John Cranko's *Pineapple Poll* from ten of Sullivan's Savoy operas serve their purpose admirably; light-operatic they may originally have been but eminently danceable they are—light concert items too, and indispensable reasons, if not the only ones, for reviving the ballets. But take another of Mackerras's arrangements (already mentioned), that of the selections from Verdi for that other Cranko ballet *The Lady and the Fool*. It is eminently danceable and a major contributor to the revivals of that ballet. Yes, but it does not live on independently because, when Verdi undoctored for a ballet is so well worth listening to, there is little point in serving up doctored Verdi apart from the ballet for which the doctoring was done. For my part I do not find this Verdi–Mackerras satisfactory. Danceable it may be but it bespeaks Italian arias and duets rather than solo-dances and *pas de deux*; that by the way.

Another comparable example: *La Fête Etrange*, for which various piano pieces and songs by Fauré have been orchestrated. This happens to be a very favourite ballet of mine, a rare instance (all the rarer since it is not a Diaghilevian product) of the blending of music, design and choreography into an enchanting unity; one in which the music is no less, though scarcely more, important than the other ingredients. This delectable ballet does seem, at first glance, to pass my 'handy test' in that the component songs, 'Soir' and 'Mandolin', and the piano pieces are certainly heard in song and piano recitals and that their orchestrated version certainly contributes a lot to the ballet's survival or revival. But really it fails; because there is no good reason why the orchestrated arrangement should be played apart from the ballet. And, just to add a complicated nuance, this ballet, when it was new, was not accompanied by orchestrated Fauré but by the pieces as Fauré wrote them, for the piano.

If you ask, as you well may, why I bother about such detailed complications I answer that I want to remind the reader, and perhaps myself as well, that the path of this attempted analysis—of what gives long life to a ballet or other dance-work—is littered with minority cases and, indeed, glaring exceptions. Music, I maintain, is the principal contributor to a ballet's longevity; but it is by no means always so. And, though it is necessary to generalize and useful to have a handy test as to the kind of music which makes this principal contribution, the test's scope is limited and the generalizations are fallible.

Choreography as preservative

Now comes an oddity: the very best of ballets have been set to music which was never intended for dancing, superb music which the given ballet has taken over quite undoctored. Odd that this should be so; but there it is and the more I look at it the surer of it I become. The oddity does not end there; for such music demands particularly meritorious choreography and the relevant ballets are not mainly kept alive by this superb music of theirs. The music will live on, where it belongs, in the concert-hall but not as an encouragement to revive or perpetuate the ballets; it is too self-sufficient for that. So the longevity of such ballets will depend mainly on the choreography. And so I arrive at the curious, melancholy conclusion that the ballets which are likely to last longest are not the very best, because choreography is more subject than music is to erosion. Another and blunt way of putting it is to say that the very best music kills choreography. And, you might add, thank goodness that if choreographers must, as they apparently must, put their hands on a Beethoven late quartet (van Manen), a Bach violin concerto (Balanchine and others), the Brandenburg Concertos (Cranko), the Beethoven Seventh, Brahms Fourth, Tchaikovsky Sixth and Berlioz's *Symphonie Fantastique* (Massine), the Bizet Symphony (Balanchine), Mahler's *Lied von der Erde* and *Kindertotenlieder* (MacMillan and Tudor), they are likely to get their fingers burnt. But that does not always happen. Out of the examples I have just given the only first degree burns are Massine's on the Beethoven Seventh Symphony, Cranko's on the Brandenburgs, and perhaps van Manen's on the *Grosse Fuge*; the others get away with it more or less and Tudor's *Dark Elegies* (*Kindertotenlieder*) and MacMillan's *Lied von der Erde* do much better than that—they are excellent ballets. After all, Massine's symphonic ballets, *Les Présages* (Tchaikovsky's Sixth), *Choreartium* (Brahms's Fourth), and the *Symphonie Fantastique* were once all the rage; it was only the last of them, to Beethoven's Seventh, which was immediately killed. Not everyone was bowled over by the others but many sincere and able critics were. These 'symphonic ballets' did, all of them, eventually wither and I cannot imagine their being revivable nowadays; but their withering took time. Will time similarly erase those we now consider good-to-excellent, such as (from the examples given) *Dark Elegies* and the *Lied*? And this question-mark hangs like a particularly unwanted ghost over the great ones—*Symphonic Variations* for instance and *Dances at a Gathering*. Will César Franck and Chopin eventually kill them too? Will their choreography be sufficiently erosion-proof for them to continue to be the balletic enhancement which they now are to their exactingly self-sufficient music?

Dance notation

If any practitioner of choreography or of the Laban system of dance notation has been reading this chapter he, or more likely she, will have been doing so with mounting exasperation. I can imagine him or her, at this point, jumping up to give furiously the answer which, according to any convinced dance notator, I should have given long ago: that, however it may have been in the past, dance notation, with or without the help of film or video-tape, can and does preserve choreography; so that it is no longer true that choreography, hitherto preserved only in the memories of choreographer and dancers, need be eroded by time. Henceforth, the argument goes on, the music will be at least rivalled, if not surpassed, by the choreography as main preservative. It may be so. Sceptical though I admit to being about the claims of dance notation, there is evidence which I too admit to be incontrovertible, that it does pass on some choreography intact. The most recent example I heard about was from Kenneth MacMillan. The West Berlin Ballet, when he was in charge of it, had put on Ashton's *Scènes de Ballet*, entirely through the good offices of a Royal Ballet trained choreologist. He had been in the cast of this ballet when it was produced at Covent Garden, remembered it well and could vouch for the accuracy of the (20 or more years later) Berlin version. Evidence incontrovertible and welcome. *Scènes de Ballet*, it might be said, is relatively simple choreologically speaking: a neo-classical exercise, close to the academic prescription and with a quite small cast. But there is plenty of corroborative evidence about bigger and more complicated works.

In any case, choreology or, for that matter, the discouragingly complicated Laban system, with or without the help of film or video-tape, cannot be written off if it fails, as yet, to fulfil the total claims sometimes made for it; it is better than nothing and, I guess, it improves all the time. Some 'ifs' remain; if some acceptable (which includes 'not prohibitively difficult') system of notation can really cope with a variety of dance styles and if that system becomes generally accepted, then the inevitable impermanence of choreography will be a thing of the past and ballets will no longer die simply because choreographer and dancers no longer remember them. We are not there yet but at least on limited fronts—one of which is that of choreology as used and propagated by the Royal Ballet—there is progress; there is now much less likelihood that *Symphonic Variations* and *Dances at a Gathering* will, like Balanchine's *Cotillon*, be lost because forgotten.

I confess to another doubt, which may or may not be rational. I fear that, with or without notation, the stylized movements of human bodies, which is another way of saying 'dance', may be more vulnerable than music is to the erosions of time, taste and fashion. Music too is not immune. I fear that choreography may be even less so. I am not suggesting that, generally and necessarily, the judgement of the eye is even less constant than that of the ear. I am suggesting it, rationally or not, only in respect of stylized human movement. Perhaps it is simply that knowing something, however inexpertly, about dance notation's history of frustration during the 19th century and about the mutual scratchings and clawings of rival systems in our own time, I still jib at believing that dance can ever have so iron-clad, irrefutable and generally recognized a system as belongs to and preserves music. Perhaps it is just a reactionary, old fogeyish hunch. At any rate it is based on a bewildered awareness of the multitudinous nuances of human gesture, from toe to fingertip, and of the acute difficulty of reducing them to an accurate, permanently decipherable record of signs and cyphers. How much easier it is to write down the sound of music!

And if that hunch of mine is irrational, there is nothing irrational about the proposition that a system of dance notation, however generally accepted, will make little difference to most ballets' real life-span on stage. Think of the size and rapid turnover of any ballet company's repertory. The only 'constants' are the half-dozen

19th century classics and very few others; for the rest, programmes
are for ever changing. Novelty is all, even though, or rather, because,
the quality of the novelty is seldom high. The reason is not that
choreography gets quickly forgotten; forgetfulness is not so quick
as all that. It is that company managements or audiences or ballet
itself (it amounts to the same thing) must have change; they must
have it even in the classics, for these 'constants' too are, time and
again, revised. A *Cotillon* would, no doubt, have been saved from
oblivion by dance notation but *Les Sylphides*, accurately recorded in
its original form, could scarcely have been revived more often than,
however inaccurately, it has been. A prospective new choreographer
of *Le Sacre du Printemps* would have the advantage of reference to
MacMillan's version, whereas MacMillan could not refer to
Nijinsky's original, but that would be most unlikely to deter the
new man from going ahead. Dance notation will fill libraries and
will rescue a few works for the stage; it will make little difference
to choreography's hectic turnover.

Exceptions, minorities, freaks

Dance notation did not begin with Laban and choreology. It has
some earlier successes among its credentials. The Sadler's Wells
Ballet's classical repertory was, after all, founded on the Stepanov
notation of *Swan Lake* etc., which Nicholas Sergeyev, one-time
regisseur at the Maryinsky, appropriated from St Petersburg and
turned into his passport to prosperity in the West. Even without
notation or with only the squiggles of a private shorthand to support
dancers' and choreographers' memories, some choreography has
survived for a very long time. Whether it has survived accurately
(which is unlikely) or as an approximation, choreography, rather
than music has, we know, kept some ballets alive. *Les Sylphides*
for instance has survived abundantly since 1908 whereas all
Fokine's other, later and once famous works have, at best, kept
going much more haltingly. That is not—or not mainly— because
of its music. Those Chopin pieces do not even now, after all
these years of *Les Sylphides*, necessarily imply the ballet; they are
self-sufficient and live entirely on their own. Is it then because
of the relationship between the music and its choreography? Yes,
certainly. But that really means: because of some enduring quality
in the choreography—and that despite Fokine's frequent reminders
to us, in his later years, that his sacrosanct work had been mangled

by successive iconoclasts and also despite the fact that, when he reproduced, as he did from time to time, what he called an authentic version, there were dancers who could tell you convincingly that the master's reproductions often differed materially from the original. Well *Les Sylphides*, authentic or bowdlerized and ill-performed as it often is, belongs to the pure dance kind of ballet —a fine example of its supreme, most balletic kind. And while its kind of choreography, if unhelped by dance notation, is no more erosion-proof than any other, it is much more likely to survive, on its basic choreographic, balletic merit than the more dramatic, more trespass-inclined works which made up the rest of Fokine's output. Those others, as I said earlier, may be revived intermittently because of their music and because they are significant choreographic relics but this one is made of the stuff which, however eroded, is ballet's very essence. I repeat: all choreography, if not written down, tends to wither and die, but this, the pure dance kind, less so than the rest.

For other examples I go back to the 19th century's *La Bayadère*, *Don Quixote*, *Giselle* and *La Sylphide*, on which I touched earlier. *La Bayadère*: you do not have to hate poor Minkus in order to be pretty sure that the big, self-contained extract from this Maryinsky three-acter (as produced by Nureyev in the West) does not really survive because of its music. The music happens to be Minkus at about his best—a tuneful, very precise servant to the choreography; and, like it or not, it is very much part of this particular whole; this humble Minkus is absolutely right for this proud Petipa. That said, it is undoubtedly the proud Petipa which keeps this extract gloriously alive; the choreography is a gem of 19th century Russian classicism, comparable with Ivanov's second act of *Swan Lake*. Everything I said above as to why and how Fokine's choreography has kept *Les Sylphides* going applies to Petipa's choreography for *Bayadère*. With two differences, however. The Minkus, unlike the Chopin, has no separate life of its own and Petipa's choreography, unlike Fokine's, is so very academic, so free of idiosyncratic nuance, that it is much easier to remember exactly and pass on, with or without notation.

Don Quixote I regard as an incorrigible freak. That it does survive in some form, all three acts of it, is undeniable—in Soviet Russia with choreography 'after' Petipa perhaps, but very distantly 'after', and in the west intermittently in various other versions, the latest of which is Nureyev's brisk and bright filmed one. Only Minkus remains fairly constant in these revivals (not, however, in

Balanchine's *Don Q*); and I refuse to believe that this cumulatively dreadful repetition of trite tunes, all with an unvarying *sforzando* and thumping, full close, is really the reason for its survival. I believe it survives as a freakish relic and because there is such a shortage of ballets nowadays, especially three-acters; and I am glad that it does so, as a reminder of what Diaghilev rebelled against. Not that he needed to rebel against the very familiar *pas de deux* of *Don Q*'s final act; to see the full three acts is to realize just why this *pas de deux* crops up again and again in gala performances whereas the remainder is, mercifully, not revived all that often.

Then there is *Giselle*: blessed with Adam's score, very serviceable and much more acceptable than Minkus, though not, I consider, independently alive. Blessed also with a much better story—more coherent, more dramatic, better balanced—than those of *Swan Lake* or *Beauty* or *Nutcracker* or any other 19th century classic you can think of; and giving a role to the male dancer which is exceptionally fine by any standards and, by comparison with any subsequent 'baroque' classic, is almost incredible. (In the romantic period, that of Bournonville and of *Giselle* itself, the male dancer was more favoured.) There, I think, you have the reasons why this ballet is the oldest of the really hardy survivors, the only one which still vies in popularity with (the younger) *Swan Lake* and *Beauty*. It has a remarkably good scenario and a pretty exact one too, which has not prevented producers from considerable tinkering and from 'discovering' ever more 'authentic' versions, but has, nevertheless, given a firm, general prescription for the main lines of the choreography. Of course, what we now have—what is available everywhere, including Paris—is derived from Petipa's Maryinsky version of the 1880s. The detailed choreography, I'd dare bet, has wandered a long way from that and there's no saying how far Petipa had already wandered from Perrot's original for Carlotta Grisi in Paris in 1842. *Giselle* then can be said to survive because of its choreography only if the meaning of choreography can be taken to include not just a precise detailing of movement but a more general prescription arising out of the scenario. In *Giselle* it is the scenario which has counted. It is one of a kind. A freak, if you like, but how much more beautiful and memorable, how much sturdier than *Don Q*. One of a kind, and yet *La Sylphide* is not dissimilar; less compelling, much less universal—having re-emerged only quite recently from its Danish incubator—and as much a Taglioni relic as a ballet kept alive by its own merit, but still preserved mainly by its ever-valid, simple, fairy-tale scenario. The Danes have been exceptionally persistent preservers of choreography—Bournonville's, that is. Impossible to swear that *Napoli, Flower Festival at Genzano* or *School of Ballet* are just as Bournonville made them but they certainly represent a long-established, continuing style which is distinct from the main Petipa–Sadler's Wells one. And no one could maintain that they or *La Sylphide* are preserved by the hotchpotches which are their musical accompaniments. 'Folk-memory', if isolated from outside influences, can be strong and true; that is why today we still have these Danish Bournonville choreographic survivals. Butterflies preserved in Danish amber.

From such minority cases—ballets without distinguished music but preserved by their choreography or scenarios, and pre-dating even the present measure of 'semi-demi-standardization' of dance notation—I return momentarily to those set to really fine, undoctored scores; the sort which, as I said before, are too self-sufficient to be identified with the ballets subsequently tacked on to them. What is notable is how many good-to-excellent ballets there are in this category. *Symphonic Variations* and *Dances at a Gathering—Les Sylphides* too, when (rarely, rarely) done well—may be my particular shining delights, but what a lot of others there are. Every one of Tudor's five memorable ballets has been accompanied by such music rather than by a specially written score, *Lilac Garden* by Chausson's *Poème, Dark Elegies* by Mahler's *Kindertotenlieder, Pillar of Fire* by Schoenberg's *Verklärte Nacht, Echoing of Trumpet*s by Martinu's *Fantasies Symphoniques* and *Shadowplay* by Koechlin's *Banderlog*. Most of Balanchine's famous works have been to Stravinsky's ballet music, but there are also his *Serenade* (Tchaikovsky's *Serenade for Strings*) and his *Liebeslieder Waltzer* (Brahms). There are MacMillan's *Song of the Earth* (Mahler) and Ashton's *Monotones* (Satie's *Gymnopoedie*) and his *Dream* (with the order of Mendelssohn's music for *A Midsummer Night's Dream* just a bit rearranged from the usual concert version). Very few of Ashton's ballets have been set to specially composed scores; most of them have taken on previously existing music, some of it rearranged for the ballet, but some not rearranged at all.

All that, though notable, is not so astonishing if we remember the range of the Diaghilevian emancipation. For Diaghilev not only persuaded distinguished composers to contribute to ballet, he virtually opened all music to the choreographer; or at least he left the door ajar for his successors to push wide open. Remember that before him all the music used by ballet was specially composed for it—hence Minkus, Pugni and Drigo as well as Tchaikovsky, Delibes and Messager—whereas after him all music was there for the choreographers to match if they dared. No surprise at all that many of them dared beyond their station and that their choreography, failing to measure up to the self-sufficient music of their choice, was killed by it. But no great surprise either that the best of them, Tudor, Ashton, Balanchine, MacMillan *et al.*, given all music to choose from, chose what inspired them to good or even great choreography.

Decor

Earlier in this chapter I gave a highly selective list of ballets which have survived because of the music composed for them. Diaghilevian ballets dominated the list and if the list had been extended that dominance would have been, if anything, even more evident. But much as Diaghilev improved ballet music, from Minkus to Stravinsky and, ultimately, to undoctored Beethoven, Bach, Brahms, Franck, Chopin, Mahler, etc., he did at least as much for the other ancillary, the designs. To what extent then, in this post-Diaghilevian era, can the decor and costumes help to preserve a ballet? The nearest equivalent to the handy test which I applied to at least some music (in trying to assess the music's contribution to a ballet's longevity) would be the value—meaning starkly, I suppose, the money value— of the original sketches; and in any such assessment the designs for Diaghilev's ballets by Picasso, Braque, Matisse, Derain, Rouault, Roehrich, Laurencin, Gontcharova, Larionov, Benois and a dozen others would be jostling each other about the top of the list. The more valuable, delectable, admirable the designs, the more they will help in preserving the related ballet. That would seem to be, on the face of it, a safe proposition. In fact, it is not so safe as all that because complications of cost and suitability come into the reckoning. Costumes may be beautiful but 'undanceable', decor may be gorgeous but prohibitively expensive to reproduce. Are Balanchine's later ballets, for instance, more likely or less likely to survive because they are dressed in plain tights and set against a plain back-cloth? More likely, in all probability, because their choreography is distinguished enough to stand up to nakedness (so to speak) and because the sparseness of their designs makes them, financially if not artistically, the more desirable. Balanchine, of course, has made

a great thing about the rightness of leaving the dancers as naked
as is decently possible, and about the wrongness of cluttering the
shape of the choreography with a lot of costumery. The dance set
to music, he has said, is what matters; let there be no distraction
from it. He has not been consistent about this and he may, partly
it not wholly, have been making an artistic virtue of economic
necessity; the NYCB during much of its career has had little cash
to spare for decor and costumes. At any rate this asceticism does put
an extra burden on the choreography; so it had better be good. All
very well for Balanchine; he may get away with it at least in the
short run, though in the long one it is questionable if some of his
choreography, too, may not suffer in general estimation for lack of
decorative distraction. How much more so the choreography of his
emulators. There can, at least, be no doubt that some designers
have greatly contributed to the longevity and the immediate success
of some ballets.

Just how much is that contribution? As much as that of the music?
One way, perhaps the only one, of answering those questions is to
take a few examples of much revived ballets to which the designs
have, clearly, been of particular importance. Take again *Le Tricorne*. It owes a lot to Picasso. But surely even more to de Falla.
Without Picasso it is imaginable, without de Falla it is not. Or *Les
Noces*; Gontcharova's contribution is a big one, making this work
an exceptionally complete, three-faceted masterpiece; but Stravinsky,
surely, contributed even more; so did Nijinska (in my opinion),
though it is not irrelevant that Robbins, discarding Gontcharova
and, of course, Nijinska, made another excellent ballet to the same
music. Gontcharova again gave much to *The Firebird*; she was not,
as it happens, its original designer (Golovine's 'originals' were soon
put aside by Diaghilev because, I think, they were too cumbersome);
and both Balanchine and Cranko have had a go at the choreography, dismissing Fokine (and Gontcharova) but keeping Stravinsky. The Fokine–Gontcharova–Stravinsky *Firebird* is, I consider,
a choreographic relic; it is really Stravinsky, helped greatly by
Gontcharova and only marginally by Fokine, who keeps it going.
Petrouchka, which once seemed choreographically extraordinary, is
a dead sensation now; and despite Benois's irreplaceable, apposite
designs, much better heard in the concert-hall than seen on stage. In
all these instances the designs have mattered a lot, but always, I
think, less than the music.

I can think of just one ballet, the Cocteau–Picasso–Satie–Massine

Parade, in which the designs (Picasso's) have indubitably mattered more than the other ingredients and have been the main reason why it has been revived at all—albeit seldom. Among long-living ballets, or those fairly often revised, there has been in my experience no such example. Indeed, I can think of only five borderline cases: ballets about which it is not really possible to be sure whether their designs or their music matters more. One of these is Ninette de Valois's *The Rake's Progress,* which was certainly *prompted* by Hogarth (that is a rather different point) and which may owe its frequent revivals by the Royal Ballet no less to Rex Whistler's Hogarth-inspired designs than to Gavin Gordon's amusing and suitable music and to de Valois's popular choreography. I am unsure about it; unsure too whether Poulenc or Laurencin contributed more to the revivability of *Les Biches* (but does *Les Biches* quite qualify as a 'frequent revival'?), or Derain or Rossini–Respighi to *La Boutique Fantasque,* or Derain again or Lecocq to *Mam'zelle Angot.* I am sure, however, that in these three ballets the music-cum-design has endured much better than, respectively, Nijinska's and Massine's choreography. My only other borderline case is the admirable *Fête Etrange* which, to my mind, owes as much to Fedorovitch as to Fauré and hardly less to Andrée Howard.

No doubt, other people could add an example or two to this scanty collection. Perhaps Bakst and Rimsky-Korsakov have shared equally in keeping *Scheherazade* intermittently alive; perhaps Rouault is to be thanked as much as Prokofiev and Balanchine for the revivals of *The Prodigal Son;* and perhaps in some of Diaghilev's later ballets which, apart from *Parade,* I have not mentioned, the designs really did count for more than either the music or the choreography (but if so, none of those particular ballets has endured). In any ballet which has endured, apart from the very occasional *Parade,* the designs have, at most and very rarely, been equal sharers with the music and sometimes with the choreography as well; the designs have never been (as the music has been often and the choreography sometimes) the indubitably main preservative. That (*pace* Balanchine) is far from saying that decor and costumes do not matter. For certain ballets, including the very best, they should, no doubt, be simple rather than luxuriant. But simplicity and unimportance are not synonyms; the right simplicity is achieved not by dismissiveness but by most attentive artistry. There is a world of difference between the simplicity of Fedorovitch and the meagreness (and vulgarity) of Karsinska. True, with minimal attention to designs you can produce a ballet of sorts, which you could not do with comparable inattention to music and choreography. Only to that extent is 'Mr B' right. (But he knows that perfectly well. He just likes to be naughty.)

Elusive identity

So I come at last to the 'supplementaries', as I called them; those questions which, early in this chapter, I put away in the store-cupboard, to be taken out and looked at in due course. When is a revival not a revival but something essentially new? How much alteration can a ballet stand and still retain its original identity? I look hard at these questions and the answer I come to is that it is quite impossible to give any nice, clear answer at all. Are the numerous versions of *Romeo and Juliet* which have been set to Prokofiev's score one and the same ballet? Surely they are not; the differences of choreography, to say nothing of design, are too great for that. And yet they do, most of them, follow one and the same scenario in pretty close detail. But then are the several versions of *The Sleeping Beauty* or *Swan Lake*, all 'after Petipa' and all using Tchaikovsky, though often not quite the same Tchaikovsky, and all using different designs—are they essentially one and the same work? And what about *The Nutcracker*, in which the only constant is the music? Is Fokine's *Firebird* essentially the same as Balan-chine's? Hans van Manen's *Daphnis and Chloe* the same as Ashton's and as Fokine's? Robbins's *Les Noces* as Nijinska's?

Well, we might be able to agree that to retain a ballet's identity both the music and the choreography have to remain more or less unchanged whereas changes, even big changes, in the designs are much less destructive. That, at least, would be my contention. For though (I repeat) I am far from arguing that the designs do not matter, they are, figuratively as well as literally, peripheral, as the music and choreography are not. That statement may seem hard to justify. For the designs must merge with the dancers' movements to make a ballet's visual element; and it might seem difficult to maintain that changes in one of the two components which form this visual whole are less important (more peripheral) than changes in the other or, indeed, than changes in the sound to which the 'visible totality' is set. But I think there are two answers which, taken together, make the point—not with irrefutable logic but 'common-sensibly': if you alter the movements (the choreography) you are altering what distinguishes ballet from any other theatrical art; this you are not doing if you alter the costumes—you will be making the choreography look somewhat different, no doubt, but not so different as all that. And if you alter the music then you are bound to alter the choreography. The choreography and the relationship between it and its music—these are intrinsic to the ballet; the designs are not. The evidence, I think, is there in my inability to call to mind more than a very few examples of works which, for their survival or revival, have depended as much on their designs as on their music and/or choreography. Again it is, I think, relevant that the choreographer's inspiration, his motivation for the ballet, is very often in the music; sometimes, admittedly, in the story or in a character, but most of all in the music—and seldom in the designs. Here we have to distinguish. There are ballets, not many but a few, which have been inspired by a painter or a picture or pictures. Thus *The Rake's Progress*, inspired by Hogarth, which I have already mentioned; and to that should be added *Job* (Blake) and *The Prospect Before Us* (Rowlandson), good ballets both and, like *The Rake's Progress*, dating from the time in the 1930s when Ninette de Valois was bravely proclaiming the Britishness of her fledgling company and hit on the excellent idea of using British painters, as a source for thoroughly British choreography. Other painters, Goya for instance, and Velasquez, have similarly prompted other ballets. But such promptings to choreography by painters or pictures do not have the immediacy or pervasive effectiveness of promptings by music; the painter's veritable work has to be transmuted into scenery and costumes by 'middle-men' (so John Piper for Blake and Whistler for Hogarth) and neither the originals nor the decor and costume suggested by them can guide the choreographer in detail, as the music can and does. Besides (this by the way), to say that the ballet was prompted by a painter is not the same as saying that the consequent designs necessarily matter more than the music to the ballet as ultimately presented. Blake prompted *Job* and Hogarth *The Rake* but Vaughan Williams, surely, and Gavin Gordon, very possibly, matter just as much to, respectively, *Job* and *The Rake* as seen on stage. And, of course, it was Cocteau's literary notions, not Picasso's designs which prompted *Parade*, but it is Picasso who makes that ballet, however infrequently, worth reviving.

Summary and postscript

How much, when all is said and done, does it matter—this inconclusive game of 'hunt the identity'? It matters just because it is so inconclusive, because far from helping us to discover what keeps a ballet alive it blurs the trail by showing how difficult—and how artificial, you might say—it is to try to pin-point a ballet's identity at all. It matters, in fact, because it reminds us of something in the very nature of ballet: that it is in a constant state of flux, that it is a three-limbed monster which for ever takes, modifies, rejects; that it is an insatiable, gluttonous, shameless, chameleon-like hybrid; and that a ballet which we see today is likely to be not quite the same tomorrow. It is nevertheless true that what keeps a ballet, however changeably, alive is first of all the music (provided the music was written or arranged for it) and after that the scenario and choreography and, last and least, the designs. It may be that dance notation is going to preserve choreography and, accordingly, make choreography a preservative comparable with the music; but we are not there yet. And, in any case, even the most generally accepted dance notation is not going to make much difference to the rapidity of the choreographic turnover. The jokers in the argument are that, on the one hand many excellent ballets, including, to my mind, the best of all, are made to music not intended for dancing and that, on the other hand, such self-sufficient music tends to kill choreography (all but the very best) rather than give long life to it. That is the sum of what I have tried to say in this chapter.

In the course of it I have said nothing whatever about modern dance-works and what preserves them. That is because what has been said about the preservation of ballet applies to them—with one difference: that their music, designs (if any) and choreography tend to be still more—much more—ephemeral. Immediacy and, consequently, a quick death are a veritable article of 'modernist' faith. In this, as in so much else, Martha Graham is the exception; she may or may not have composed for posterity (she would say that she had not) but I would bet that *Primitive Mysteries* and, perhaps, others would last and (again an exception or at least a minority case) would owe their longevity to their choreography, not to their adequate music and imaginative costumes.

Nor have I said anything about the durability of choreography which is sustained by no music at all. Marie Rambert, for one, has argued that choreography should be entirely a thing in itself, not dependent on, or necessarily allied to, music; and there are several examples of such 'unaccompanied' ballets or other dance-works. But choreography's potentiality is much more enriched than limited by music. The music prescribes the dancers' movements and therefore limits them—yes; but it also provides an *aide-mémoire* of the dance pattern without which that pattern would have to be either quite haphazard or much simplified. All in all, it is the absence of music which really limits the choreography's range, richness, elaboration and makes its life meaner and shorter. There are intermediate situations between the use of music as an exact, note-by-note or at least phrase-by-phrase accompaniment to the movement (the traditional way and still the most usual and by far the most rewarding) and its total absence; nowadays music is sometimes used, by modern dance particularly, as a mere background of noise— electronic squawks and rumbles very often—to which the movement is very loosely attached. But the closer the attachment the richer, more elaborate the dance pattern can dare to be; the more independent the choreography the more restricted—or shapeless— its inventions. And there is the further point which, perhaps, I should have noted first of all: that ballet, or any dance-work, without music is ballet deprived of what should be one of its three enchantments. Unaccompanied or even loosely accompanied choreography can only be a wayward experiment; sometimes amusing, clever, adroit but never counting for much; a signpost to a dead-end.

FIVE

Dancers

The 'X' Factor

What makes a good ballet, what the art of ballet does best or worst, why some ballets last, why others die—these things can be argued with some hope, not altogether illusory, of arriving at agreement. A persuasively objective opinion about the disembodied art of ballet can perhaps be reached. But ballet is not disembodied, not abstract; and when it comes to judging the bodies plus personality which turn the abstraction into a living performance it becomes much harder to prevent objectivity from quitting the judgement seat. Perhaps this is all because of sex. A Freudian might say so; and an erudite Freudian might be able to prove it to his own and my satisfaction. Well, bodies plus personality are the instruments of choreography; they are what ballet is distinctively about; and bodies plus more or less of personality *are* sex. You do not have to be a psychoanalyst to realize that, if you are heterosexual and the dancer is of the opposite sex (or of yours if you are homosexual), then sexual attractiveness is one big reason why you find her (him) worth watching. Other attributes come into it; of course they do and they matter as much or more. Yet perhaps these other attributes are not really other at all; perhaps your judgement of their worth is, however little you may realize it, also coloured, even governed by sexual quirks, fancies, obsessions, inhibitions and what not. But those refinements, if we were to try to sort them out, would take us deep into the psychological labyrinth where I, for one, would be lost; and, if they are not a lot of nonsense, they would carry implications about our judgement of dancers of our own as well as of the other sex; they would bring in devious complications galore.

My business, for the moment, is only with the sexual attractiveness of a dancer of the opposite sex, and how that affects judgement; a less complicated business. When the attractiveness is sex bomb-like many are susceptible to it; the fall out from a sex bomb is ubiquitous. Short of that, however, it is wonderful how much we all differ about sexual attractiveness. Nothing, but nothing, is so idiosyncratic. And it is this idiosyncratic 'X' which makes me prefer one dancer of the opposite sex and you another when otherwise there is not a pin of difference between their respective merits; whereas, because of this 'X', we are likely to disagree about their other merits as well. Again without venturing into the psychological maze, I think it follows (not for all but for some of us) that our judgements about dancers of our own sex are liable to be less fervent. And perhaps clearer headed; but of that I am not sure. I can only speak for my imperfect self and I know that, willy-nilly, I am less interested in male dancing; so perhaps my judgement suffers on both counts—too fervent about the Giselles and therefore blind to their faults, lack-lustre about the Albrechts and therefore unobservant of their merits. I hope not, but it may be so. Yet I can at least recognize that my myopia is not shared by all; and that ardent judgements about the merits of ballerinas are not confined to male 'heteros' and lesbians; nor are comparably ardent judgements about the Albrechts, Siegfrieds and the rest of the balletic male line royalty confined to women and male homosexuals. Other attributes matter.

They matter to me, too. About them there may be fairly general agreement, up to a point. There is, after all, a more or less common denominator of qualities and skills which, most of us would agree, go to make a perfect or outstanding dancer, even though a world of disagreement remains about the order of priority of these requirements. But whether we take our personal, idiosyncratic preferences at their face value or adduce hidden motives for them, there they are, making one of us put the highest premium on line, another on musicality, another on virtuosity, yet another on neatness of footwork. And I am unaware or un-Freudian or pig-headed enough (or all three) to believe that, about these skills and qualities, or rather about the proportions in which they need to be mixed, persuasion, based on experience, is worth a try. It may be possible that one man's preferences—prejudices if you like—will widen horizons, will open eyes to points previously missed or undervalued. There is, of course, no such creature as a perfect dancer; there are only those who, however imperfect, seem wonderful. I shall try to note the qualities which seem to me necessary and relate them to dancers who, some more, some less, have seemed wonderful to me.

The women: line

Line and lightness I have mentioned (chapter 2) as the particular aims of the classical technique. If one of the two has priority in the training, that one is line. Both very good line and considerable lightness, or a convincing semblance of it, are essential to the best dancers. Line encompasses a lot; not only the 'turnout' in every posture and movement, but also the tautness and flexibility of the back, the carriage of the head, the stretch and again flexibility of the arms—everything, in short, which makes for visual harmony in one dancer or in a pair or in a group of them, whether moving or in repose; and a dancer's God-given physical proportions have much to do with it. Fonteyn's line has been so beautiful partly because she was rigorously trained and had, besides, an instinct for it (that comes into it as well) but also because she was, balletically, so well proportioned—legs supple and long but not too long, a marvellously strong yet pliant back, lissome and sufficiently long arms (not sharp, not pudgy) and an erect, piquant set of neck and head. Given all this, plus training plus application she could not go wrong as to her line; and the result was a never-ending satisfaction in the eye of the observer, unstrained, harmonious. Yet, Fonteyn apart, the dancers who have delighted me most are not necessarily those whose line has been best; the most satisfactorily linear have, sometimes, seemed otherwise deficient and some whose line has occasionally been an affront have more than compensated in other ways. I say, 'whose line has occasionally been an affront' but as to that, or to lightness or musicality (about musicality I shall have much to say), I must emphasize that the standards by which I am judging are very high. That said not to exalt my standard of judgement but to serve as a reminder that all ballet dancers of quality have pretty good line; the distinction is not between pass marks and failure but between scholarship class and second-class honours or thereabouts.

I do not think I have seen another dancer, including Fonteyn, whose line has enchanted me so much as Jennifer Penney's. She too has the quite unfair gift of well-nigh perfect physical propor-

tions, plus an even more unfair prettiness; and I think (without
having had the chance to measure) she has just a little more than
Fonteyn's relative length of leg and arm, so that the line is that
much more effortlessly telling. And she, even more than Fonteyn,
seems to have been born 'turned out'. She has her limitations;
notably a lack of versatile expressiveness, which has little to do with
technique and training but counts for much. Antoinette Sibley has
excellent line, though I find it less 'life-enhancing' than Penney's;
a matter, I think, of physical proportions. Her arms are long and
very well controlled but her legs are shortish—fine beneath a *tutu*
but otherwise a bit ordinary. Anyway the great and increasing
pleasure her dancing has given me has not come primarily from her
line but, always, from the exceptionally lucid articulation of her
footwork (she has the neatest and most voluble feet of them all);
from that and more recently from her most delicate, detailed interpretation of whatever the role may be. I and others used to regard
her as a classicist solely but no actress. Her growth by study has
delightfully confounded us.

Yet as to her line, she does have one quality which I find
bewitching. I call it 'the gift of tallness' and it is due, in the first
instance, to her length of arm, though not to that only, for this
gift belongs not to all relatively long limbed dancers but only to
the very few who can use this length of limb to special effect. I
think it has to do with line though I am not quite sure that it is not
something quite separate. Certainly it is distinctive. What I mean by
this 'gift of tallness' is the telescopic ability of some dancers to
elongate, give amplitude to a movement so that it takes on an
unexpected significance. Put like that it may not sound so very
eye-catching, so rewarding; but it is a gorgeous thing when you
see it. And, yes, it *must* be an attribute of line. Paradoxically or not
it belongs not to dancers who actually are tall but to those of no
more than average height and, especially, to the small even the very
small ones and (I repeat) only to very few of whatever stature. It is
not that the line of tall dancers is unattractive; its absolute length
does make it very attractive, to me at least. Attractive but unsur-
prising. The point about 'the gift of tallness' is the delectable shock
of it; the astonishment that a creature so diminutive can so encompass space. You expect neatness, precision, speed, virtuosity
from the small ones; you do not expect this generosity of movement,
this largesse. Sibley is petite and because of her length of arm, plus
some incalulable instinct or whatever and despite her relative short-

ness of leg, she has it. So, pre-eminently has Merle Park, who is
even shorter than Sibley but relatively longer of leg as well as arm;
she, as it happens, is relatively 'turned in', getting only second-class
honours (no scholarship) for academic standard of line. Fonteyn
certainly has, or had, it. So has the Russian Makarova, who is
smaller and can look taller than almost any of them. But then
Makarova has pretty well everything (bar musicality), except for
those, not including me, who find her extrovert, confident stage-
personality somehow rebarbative: anti-Makarovites do exist. Russian
or Russian-trained dancers are, I think, blissfully likely, or used to
be, to possess this elusive gift; Russian training produces, or used to
produce, an amplitude of style and, even though the Russian
influence nowadays has become more pervasive, this 'grandeur of
amplitude' has remained till recently a Bolshoi–Kirov near-pre-
rogative. Even so it is not quite what I am talking about. The gift
of telescopic tallness is not national but personal. Another, lesser
(non-Russian) dancer who has it is Alfreda Thorogood who, for
her height, is quite exceptionally long limbed; so much so that I
rather think her physical proportions are at the limit beyond which
the relative length of limb becomes not a life-enhancing vision but
a grotesque. Moderation in all things, even in exaggeration. Nevertheless, having declared that line depends largely on physical proportions plus turnout, I have gone on to say that a very special
pleasure, not quite separable from the pleasure given by admirable
line, is to be got from certain dancers who are not at all impeccably
'turned out' and whose length of limb is quite disproportionate to
their height. So, without apology, it goes. Try as you may to work
out rules and attach labels, dancers, and the pleasure they give, will
not conform; the pleasure, like the dancers, is anarchistically
human.

The women: lightness

To dance on point is, even more than being turned out, a ballet
dancer's distinction. And on point she becomes lighter as well as,
obviously, taller. Here is the main reason why ballet dancers, as a
rule, are smallish rather than tallish. The small ones on point
become tall; the tall ones become giantesses across the footlights and
hard to match with a suitably tall partner. It tends to become
Hobson's choice: either a pair of giants, and that looks odd, or a
giantess with a dwarfed partner, and that looks odder. Truly ballet

is a small girl's world. But to lightness again: to stand on point is to seem that much more weightless, that much less earth-bound; not quite winged but not quite an ordinary human plodder. So point-work symbolizes and epitomizes ballet's striving towards the un-attainable ideal of winged weightlessness. But point-work is by no means the whole of it. Ballet dancers must jump; not only jump high but give an impression of effortless soaring. A counsel of un-obtainable perfection. But they must achieve the best approximation they can. This they do in various ways. Some, who are irremediably poor jumpers, do it by a kind of technical trickery so that by their posture in jumping (it comes to that), they seem to be jumping higher than they are. Fonteyn has been one of those. But I must stress that, though some dancers can make you forget that they are not really jumping high at all, this is not a wholly satisfactory sub-stitute for the veritable 'elevation' achieved by some others. When Ann Jenner of the Royal Ballet does a *jeté* you do not have to make allowances. It is the real thing and accordingly more rewarding than the substitute, however stylishly performed, by a dancer who is no great natural jumper. Natural jumpers often seem to pay for it, I do not know quite why, by a certain untidiness; they seldom seem to be the neatest of dancers. Thus Jenner, who soars and bounces so effortlessly, has, sometimes, messy feet. So, often, have the high-jumping Russians.

Lightness and lifting or, more accurately, being lifted: these are obviously interrelated. True that the credit for those immense lifts which are the climax of so many *pas de deux*—the jewel in the crown of virtuosity—belongs mainly not to the ballerina but to her partner; and it is the business of the partner to try to lift a not-so-light ballerina as though she were thistle-down. But even if he is as stalwart as only Bolshoi-males have tended to be, what a difference it makes when she really is light and when we wonder, primarily and instinctively, not at his concealed or almost concealed effort but at her cloud-aspiring weightlessness. A distinction without a difference? Not quite so. It is a matter of what claims our first instinctive atonishment. A hard world, indeed, for the girl who is big-boned and tall.

The women: musicality

I do not think that any good, still less great, dancer is really unmusical. Spessivtseva I never saw. We do not have to accept

Diaghilev's judgement—tilted as it was by possessiveness—that she and Pavlova were two sides of the same apple but that the Spessivtseva side was the one kissed by the sun. She was, however, a great dancer. Everyone who saw her, including the pre-eminently musical Frederick Ashton, testifies to that. Yet she was unmusical, they say. I do not quite believe it. Her musicality, no doubt, only warranted pass marks and was no match for her line, which was her supreme quality. Such dancers I have certainly known—we all have—who, without equalling Spessivtseva, delighted us in other ways but whose feeling for the music was more or less elementary, getting by most of the time if not always, though not contributing noticeably to our pleasure. The Royal Ballet's Nadia Nerina, with her marvellously strong technique and her charming bounciness, was one of those. But, at the worst, provided the dancers concerned are really good, the years of training and rehearsal create a habit of time-keeping which, by the standards of ordinary mortals, rules out rank unmusicality. Musicality may be the least of their natural aptitudes but, to a workable degree, they acquire it. Nevertheless there are empires of difference between those who can passably keep time, or even whose faithfulness to the music's beat and rhythm is blameless, and those others, the cherishable few, whose sense of movement to music is a natural benediction and a positive contributor to their fascination.

To my mind this quality counts for more than any other. I appreciate that, although few could fail to value it highly, not everyone would put it, as I do, on the highest pedestal; some would put a bigger price on line, for instance, or neatness of footwork or 'elevation'. Nevertheless I would justify its pride of place, rather than accept that here is just another quirk of personal prejudice, by saying that to move to music is, after all, the essence of dancing.

Or is it? I may have little use for dance unaccompanied by music —this I showed in my preceding chapter—and not much more for dance which employs music as a mere background of sound, a mood-setter against which the dance goes its own more or less separate way. Yet in the modern idiom rather than in ballet, but in ballet too, such dance exists; account must be taken of it. Yes, but the supremely musical dancers whom I have in mind do not or would not shed this gift of theirs, even if no sound or the most remotely relevant grunts and bangs accompanied them. Intuition perhaps, rather than demonstrable evidence makes me sure of this, for such dancers are seldom if ever to be found in works which

impose this egregious test. But sure of it I am. For these are the
dancers whose movements are music made visible; they have an easy,
irresistible, reassuring authority over rhythm, cadence and inflec-
tion; they so link, elide and separate phrases that musical pleasure
is enhanced, never jarred; they convey a sense of musical texture
and volume by a gesture's pencil stroke or by its full-coloured
abundance; and, I suppose, the test which only they pass and which
distinguishes them is that, rather than obeying the prescription of
composer and choreographer, they seem to be inventing the music
as they go along; it seems to belong to them. It follows that they
can take liberties with the score, introducing their own *rubato*,
reading its rhythms a little differently, as others would not dare;
they can take these liberties because they persuade us the music
is theirs. Whatever may have been added by training they are the
most natural of nature's dancers; either they are congenitally blessed
with this gift or they are not blessed with it at all; training cannot
give it to them. They are the dancers for whom, more than for any
others, dance seems a natural form of self-expression.

I do not mean that these, the most naturally expressive, necessarily
become the dancers with the widest range of expressiveness. That
must depend largely on technical mastery; and a relatively unmusical dancer (Nerina, Spessivtseva) may well have the sort of
physique which is more amenable to rigorous training. Among
contemporary ballerinas, those Soviet-trained wonders, Maximova
and Makarova, are surely as unmusical as Spessivtseva is said to
have been; yet there is surely none to surpass, or equal, them in
beautifully balletic, trainable and trained physique. Nor are the
most 'musical' movers necessarily the finest actresses of dance. An
ability to act-through-dance, though it has much to do with an
instinct for timing, bespeaks imagination, potentiality for cerebral
and emotional involvement, whereas the gift of musical movement
can be all unaware and has nothing to do with mind or, for that
matter, with heart. Yet as to range of expressiveness, this elusive
quality or fusion of qualities which I am trying to pin-point does,
thank goodness, go sometimes with a physique which can endure
and reward rigorous training; and, as to acting, the more closely
the details of a wordless drama are tied to the music (and such are
likely to be the best of that kind of ballet), the more this gift of
musical movement or, synonymously, of natural self-expression
through dance, is likely to be transmuted into a convincing interpretation of the given role. I have stressed that this gift is God-given.

Now I stress that its beauty, though unconcealable, is stunted unless its possessor is highly trained; it needs technique to make it flower.

I have known a few wonderfully musical dancers. Much the most famous of them is Fonteyn, about whose musicality, as one of the two special ingredients in the charm of her dancing, I wrote at length in another book nearly 20 years ago. (About the other ingredient I shall say more later in this chapter.) Her musicality has not, since then, deserted her. Far from it; it has had to work overtime. It used to crown her accomplishments; now it has become a substitute. And if it is true that it was always an alternative, a better one in my opinion, to the flights of virtuosity of which she never claimed to be capable, the difference is that her technique, though not that of a virtuoso, used to be beautifully efficient, whereas now a lot is technically beyond her. The substitute has become too evident, a conjuring trick, a circumvention rather than a fulfilment. A sad thing to see if you knew her as she used to be. But how relaxing and invigorating, how satisfying, it once was when from the moment she came on stage she emanated a three-faceted felicity: a huggable personality, an assurance of stylistic fastidiousness and this serene, inviolable unity with the music. I have said that some very musical dancers can convincingly take liberties with the tempo and the phrasing. No doubt she too could have done so, but it would not have been in keeping with the unostentatiousness which was, and is, part of her charm; she just seemed musically, absolutely, always right. So she still seems occasionally, just as her once impeccable line can still be a joy when little strain of technical ambitiousness is put on it. And that is enough, I dare say, when added to the glamour of her reputation, to reward people who did not know her before; but all too little for those who did.

About Baronova's musicality I am only less sure because it is so long—over 35 years—since I saw her dance. My fallible memory has retained (touched up perhaps) lovely images of her in musical movement. Riabouchinska, technically more limited, was another 'musical mover' of those far off de Basil days; she, as I remember, was an embodied *scherzo*, with the speed and fluidity which went so well with the third movements of Massine's then fashionable *Présages* and *Choreartium*. I think Ulanova was very musical, even in the decline of her career, before which time none of us in the west saw her. Ulanova apart, I find myself fretfully uncertain about the musicality of Soviet-trained dancers, partly because some of the music to which they perform is abysmal (think of Khatchaturian's

Spartacus) and more generally because Soviet notions of dance-tempo and phrasing seem so peculiar to my eye and ear. But that puts it too politely. For I do not really think the view (not mine only, but shared with almost every non-Soviet balletgoer) that Soviet dancers are trained to do horrid things to the *tempi* of the classics (for instance) can be dismissed as western prejudice. That they often dance across, not with, the beat of the music might, I grant, be regarded sometimes as a permissible national habit rather than a national failing, ugly though it may seem to western eyes and ears; but there can be no such exoneration for the pervasive Soviet custom of drastically slowing down the *tempi* prescribed by (for example) Tchaikovsky. I have questioned, specifically, the musicality of those superb Soviet dancers, Maximova and Makarova. Maximova may be excused as never having had the chance to know better; but Makarova has now had five western years in which to slough off her Soviet-trained unmusicality; she has not done so. The ailment is national but individual sufferers from it do not deserve to be exonerated if, like Makarova or, for that matter, Nureyev, they have been given the chance to learn more musical ways.

Our own delicious Sibley is musical but not to be put among the cherishable few; her musicality, though seldom if ever to be faulted, does not have the serene inevitability of, for instance, Monica Mason's, though in other ways her dancing has more allure. And this reminds me that some dancers whom I do not regard as exceptionally musical have, nevertheless, given me moments of the very keenest musical pleasure. So Sibley in the Dorabella variation of Ashton's *Enigma Variations*; so again Penney in that upside-down reflection in the water episode ('of Youth' it is called) in Mac-Millan's *Song of the Earth*. In these instances—there are many others as well—the choreographer has perfectly blended the dancer's style, looks, personality with a memorable score; the magic of such moments is complex but musical movement is, I think, the heart of it. Similarly but differently, Jane Landon, an unusually tall dancer who used to grace the Royal Ballet's second (big) company before she went to Germany and there, all too soon, gave up ballet, had an easy liquidity of classical style which intermittently delighted me by its musical aptness. A great dancer? She was not that; but tall girls do quite often have her sort of long limbed fluency (it is one of the few balletic 'perks' which go with tallness) and she had it more than most. Nor, I suppose, will the name of Carolyn Adams be known to many or, indeed, any outside the inner ring. She is a dancer in Paul Taylor's (modern style) company which is not one I greatly care for; and I have never seen its members, Carolyn Adams included, take on choreography which was really taxing. All the same, when I saw her some four years ago on a small stage in New London, Connecticut, the musical ease of her dancing was a gem, not quite hidden by choreographic dross. She is part-negress and negroes have rhythm—how they have it! Thus the Dance Theatre of Harlem, to which belongs the distinction of being the world's first black ballet company, may be a bit casual as to classical technique but I have never seen a white company which was, collectively, so blessed with musical fluency.

I have left my musical favourite till last. Of all the dancers who have pleased me by their musicality the one (a white one) who has pleased me most, and most often, is Merle Park. She is bolder (more arrogant if you like) than Fonteyn used to be in her treatment of the score. I have known her take liberties with *tempo* and phrasing, but not by accident or in unawareness; rather because in some subconscious way she knew better—not necessarily better for everyone, but better for her. I have never known any dancer who made such seemingly natural terpsichorean magic of her music. How does she do it? By the interaction of a negro-like physical liquefaction and, I suppose, an exceptionally acute ear. Seeing how high I rate musicality among a dancer's attributes this might seem to imply that I find her every interpretation happiest of them all; not so. Her musical touch never fails but it does not necessarily obliterate faultiness in characterization or in line. So, in *Symphonic Variations*, that supreme example of linear plus musical choreography, she is less satisfactory than the less musical but more classically shaped, more turned out, Sibley; Fonteyn used to be better still. But Park is probably the most natural dancer, by grace of physique and musicality, of all those who have topped or nearly topped the Royal Ballet. Decidedly not the best at everything but the one who communicates most instinctively by movement-to-music.

Another way of looking at it

Line, lightness, including an ability to jump and, above all, the two-faceted gift of physical fluency plus musical sense—these then seem to me to be the main armament of the finest dancers. I would add to that short list the articulate neatness of footwork which is so conspicuously exemplified by Sibley; and I would add the gift of

tallness. But now I turn the coin over. Having considered the
requisite qualities and then illustrated them by dancers I have
known, I shall now look, first, at the dancers who have pleased me
most and then consider how rich or poor they are in the listed
essentials. This may not give an entirely different result but illogi-
cally, vexingly it does not give quite the same one.

No illogicality of preference occurs about Merle Park. I have
rated fluency of musical movement as the most desirable quality
of all; she has it pre-eminently and because of it I love her dancing.
If, as I have noted, her line is less than immaculate, you can set
against that her virtuosity, her gift of tallness and her lightness;
she used not to be but has become an excellent, easy jumper and a
diamond-hard virtuoso. Baronova, I am fairly sure, was extremely
musical; about her line I am less sure, not because I suspect it was
deficient but because I do not recall exactly enough. I recall, however, that in her adolescence (one of the baby ballerinas, remember)
which was when she reached the peak of her precocious career, she
was almost chubby, decidedly earth-bound and could not jump for
toffee, though she did have a lovely length of arm and leg, the
telescopic gift of tallness. But, at the last, the reasons why her
dancing delighted me cannot be dissected like that; her technical
and other qualities came into the reckoning, of course, but so did
her failings and so did the sum of these things and then something
more as well—I mean the whole 'Baronova personality' as it emanated from the stage. So perhaps it was a matter of that elusive,
intrusive 'X' again, that idiosyncratic sex appeal which colours all
our judgements of dancing. I do not know. I do know, however,
that the pleasure given me by some dancers does seem to be dissectable; the pleasure given by others much less so. Park is of the
former sort; Baronova, Fonteyn and, perhaps, Sibley of the latter.

This brings me to 'the other ingredient' in Fonteyn's dancing to
which, earlier in this chapter, I referred in passing. It is not merely
that personality counts for much, for or against, in a dancer's
power to delight but that the personalities of some dancers, their
stage-personalities at least, seem to alter in the course of their
careers, whereas others seem immutable. My hunch (after 40 years'
experience it is still only a hunch) is that the really great ones are
the 'immutables'. All good dancers have a wonderful quality when
they are young; when it has already become clear that they are
more than ordinarily proficient but their technique has not yet been
fully developed, hardened, into steely exactitude. It is an April

quality. Perhaps it is no more than that, the irresistible, dewy attractiveness of talented youth. But it is, somehow, more personal than that implies. It is the as yet untarnished, unbuffeted 'self' which they bring to their dancing. As they progress in technical efficiency many seem to lose it; indeed, almost all of them and especially those who grow into virtuosi. It seems to me that the greatest are those who do not lose it, who through all those years of advance from *coryphée* to soloist to ballerina to perhaps *assoluta*, keep this initial personality of theirs intact. For it is certainly true that those who are admired not for what they 'do' but for what they 'are' last better. (And don't tell me that this distinction, between 'being' and 'doing', which in life is blurred enough, becomes blurred beyond recognition in dance, where the particle of 'being' is embedded in a huge amount of 'doing'. The distinction holds; not with a logician's precision but, I suggest, as a signpost through territory which would be a logician's despair.) A virtuoso's life is short; the enduring dancer is one from whom emanates something other than an impression of sheer skill, even including the natural, unaware skill of musicality. An April quality I have called it; it has to do with 'vulnerability'; and yet it is also an invulnerable essence of personality, a permanence, as I have said, of 'self'.

I suppose that the only dancer who serves me as an absolutely sure illustration is Fonteyn, because she is the only one, reputed great, whom I have seen from the April of her career to its late autumn; and she is certainly the dancer of all dancers who has been loved, is loved still through the clouds of legend and publicity, for what she is rather than for what she does. There is about her still the essence of that personality which was there in her first Giselle at Sadler's Wells in 1937.

Another top ballerina of the Royal Ballet whom I have known from early days till autumn is Beriosova; a much loved heiress apparent whose bad luck it has been that the Queen (Fonteyn) had extraordinary staying power whereas she had not. So her time as all-purpose ballerina (recently she has made do with character roles) was spent in that gentle but formidable shadow. Her arabesques, some say, have been all her technical equipment. A quite unjustified slur, of course, but one which points to a truth; her technique, for so exalted a dancer, was limited. Like Fonteyn, but much more so, she succeeded not by virtuosity but by personality. For my part I have always loved her dancing but, so long as she was still taking ballerina roles, affection was fraught with increasing anxiety because she herself was so obviously anxious lest her technique was not enough to see her through. I have loved her best at the beginning and at what seems to be the end: when she was all fresh with her very own April quality (at once so cool, so reserved and so passionate) and brimful, as it then seemed, of rare promise; and later on when she was reconciled to characterizations which made little or no technical demands on her but through which she expressed an adult femininity, a most lovable womanliness, rare—indeed unique—in the stars of ballet. She, conspicuously, 'is' rather than 'does', with the melancholy difference that the requisite amount of 'doing' has been, technically and temperamentally, too much for her.

About others it is much more a matter of my instinct and my guessing. Baronova 'was' as well as 'did'; but then, you may rightly say, Baronova, when she was marvellous and when I saw her, was so very young—who knows how she would have developed through a long career? My guess, however, is that she had the sort of inviolable personality which lasts. Ulanova, I suspect, had it too; certainly when I saw her in her decline (and I did not see her before that), there was more to her, on stage I mean, than the dissectable total of her physical and technical attributes. Perhaps it had to do with a fairly obvious, physical handicap of hers—a hunched back in the midst of all those characteristically and rightly lauded super-straight, imperious Russian backs; perhaps she had had to work super-hard to create in us, her audience, the illusion that her back was not hunched at all (Taglioni, remember, is said to have been similarly hunched, or round shouldered). Again I—all of us in the west—saw little of her, so I cannot do more than guess that the distinctive Ulanova-personality which she emanated late in her career was as it had always been; but she did seem to be one who 'was' rather than 'did'. Yet again, I am suspicious of the memories I cherish of her dancing because, as luck had it, I saw her dance in Florence on her very first appearance in the west, before any other British critic had the same good fortune; and I am not sure but that this gave me a smug, proprietary interest in her 'greatness'. When, four years later, she came with the Bolshoi to Covent Garden, I know that, though still finding her special amid the cohorts of straight-backed Bolshoi talent, I admired her rather less. Well, she was four precious years older by then; but she had also become common London property, no longer only mine.

I do not find anything quite so personally distinctive in
Maximova or Makarova, the two other Soviet dancers who have
given me most pleasure. Both I have seen as much as (Makarova
much more than) I saw Ulanova. Both, apart from the Soviet mal-
formation of their musical sense, seem wonderfully capable of anything that ballet can ask of them; but have they more than that?
About Maxinova, with her irrepressibly coquettish stage-sensuality,
I could well be wrong; I wish I had seen her dance more often.
Among our own current best dancers Sibley has it rather than Park,
or at least the one has retained an air of frailty, of endearing vulnerability, through all her years of technical progress, whereas, as I
mentioned earlier, the other has become a diamond-hard virtuoso;
and about that, however stunning, there is something chilly and
impersonal. Lynn Seymour has been the most conspicuous personality of them all at Covent Garden; gifted with a rippling
suppleness of movement, thoroughly musical (I am sure she is that),
a dancer whose poignant or comic acting could touch your heart—
and withal a unique, almost an idiosyncratic stage-presence. I have
a mental image of her at Covent Garden, from more than 15 years
ago, when she was dancing the Dawn variation in the last act of
Coppelia; all the soft gamine Seymour otherness was there, even in
that minor classical solo. Her personality did not change but, alas,
her physique did. I can appreciate that for some people, jaded by the
copperplate neatness and reticence of the typical good Royal Ballet
dancer, her flamboyant, defiant non-conformity was irresistible. For
me, however, her physical and therefore technical limitations—and
her visible though not emotional or psychological unsuitability to a
lot of roles—hindered enjoyment from quite early in her career. She
is the most richly endowed of them all and the one on whom fate,
in the form of fatness, played a dirty trick. But recently, as once
before, briefly, six years ago, it seemed as though at last she had
beaten the enemy. The Seymour who was the Royal Ballet's very
frequent 'guest-ballerina' in 1975 was svelte, slim (but not thin),
lighter than she had ever been and dancing as never before—the
inimitable fluency enhanced by a new technical mastery and by a
new length and clarity of line. And she looked no older than when,
in 1960, she first astonished us all in *The Invitation*. All this at the
age of 36 and with three children—a renaissance indeed. Long may
it endure.

A favourite of mine whom, so far I have not mentioned, is
Marcia Haydée, the Brazilian ballerina of Stuttgart. I discovered her

late; not till she came with the Stuttgart company to Covent Garden
in the summer of 1974. I had quite often seen her before; but only
when, in the space of a few weeks here, I discovered the range of
her capability, for comedy, tragedy, the straight classical, the classical with a modern twist to it or carrying various degrees of drama
or whimsy—only then were my eyes really opened to her. An extraordinary and lovable dancer in whose performances, late though I
was to realize it, there is and, I am now sure, must always have been,
a common denominator, that of intellectual as well as emotional
integrity. 'Intellectual' is not an adjective which jumps to mind
about many dancers; not in my experience about any of the best
except her. Not that her dancing suggests a blue-stocking; but it
does, somehow, put across a thoughtful, aware as well as emotional
person. Her discoverer, John Cranko, said, with a courtier's grace,
the true word: 'Marcia cannot be pretty, she is much too beautiful
for that.' She is not pretty; too sharp limbed and sharp featured,
with an expression which, but for her dark, eloquent eyes, might
be forbiddingly school-marmish. Until you know her, that is, on
stage or off it; then her personality comes through and is not
school-marmish at all, but warm, sensitive, rational. Not, like
Ulanova's back, a victory won over a handicap but the truth of a
personality brushing aside, effortlessly, the first superficial impression. Though she looks at first as though she might be, she is not
one of your steely virtuosi; in that she is quite like Fonteyn used to
be—up to all the technical demands but no dazzler. She is certainly
musical and, as a dance-actress, the only one I know who is as convincing as Seymour; as convincing and more versatile. But her
dancing conveys more than the sum of these attributes; she is one of
the undissectables.

Curious, perhaps, that this Europeanized Brazilian is the only
transatlantic ballerina so far mentioned by me. Yet not so curious if
it is borne in mind that I am trying, not to draw up a world team,
an international first eleven, of the best ballerinas but to illustrate
some notions of mine, right or wrong, about dancers. The illustrations may include—I hope they do—dancers recognized as being, or
having been, among the very best. But the main reason why most
of them—and particularly so many members of the Royal Ballet—
are there among my illustrations is that they are the dancers best
known to me either now or sometime in the past 40 years. That does
not explain my more than passing references to the transcendent
Russians, Ulanova, Maximova and Makarova; they are there because

their impact, if not all that frequent, has been, to put it mildly, special.

I have seen many ballerinas of American (U.S.) companies but not, alas, the young, evidently superb Gelsey Kirkland; or at least, not since 1970 when she was *very* young. I have greatly liked Nora Kaye for her dancing-acting (memorably in *Fall River Legend*), Mimi Paul for her lithe sensuality (a most un-Balanchinesque dancer in Balanchine's company, she used to be), the famous Alicia Alonso (but she is Cuban) and the charming Violette Verdy (but she is very French). Suzanne Farrell I recognize as the epitome of all the qualities of a Balanchine ballerina; which means that a quality she does not demonstrate, and one I am always hungry for, is that of personality. Rosella Hightower's amazing virtuosity, Marjorie Tall-chief's gentle elegance—these have, respectively, overwhelmed me and won me, in their time. Of them all the one who stays with most delectable obstinacy in my memory is the other and more renowned Tallchief—Maria. I remember her for her imperturbable technical prowess and, especially, her beautifully proportioned, athletic phy-sique; a dancer who looked gorgeous off-stage as well as on it; a memorable vision but not an illustration relevant to my present text.

The men

I turn to the men. At the beginning of this book I mentioned that I saw Leonide Massine on my very first visit to the ballet, at the Alhambra in 1933. I said he was unrivalled by any male dancer I had seen since and I implied, if I did not quite state, that as the Hussar in his own *Beau Danube*, he made a more memorable impression on me than did any of the gorgeous young ballerinas in that first programme of mine. (This by way of suggesting that my myopic concentration on the ballerinas has not been so absolute as all that.) Massine was the cancan dancer in his own *Boutique Fantasque* rather than an Albrecht; the Charlie Chaplin-like Bar-man in his (lost) *Union Pacific* rather than a Prince Siegfried, the Miller in his *Tricorne* rather than a Prince Florimund; in short, a character-dancer rather than a pure classicist. And with one recent exception, to whom I shall come later, it is true that I have enjoyed his dancing of 30–40 years ago more than any other man's; also that I have got more pleasure from others of his kind than from the *danseurs nobles*, or their latter-day equivalents, however brilliant.

But before you, or I, conclude that this tells more about me and my myopia than it does about male ballet dancing in our time, we should pause. Balanchine once said and, poor man, he has never been allowed to forget it: 'Ballet is a woman's world, where man is the honoured guest.' Putting aside the flip rejoinder that in many of Balanchine's own works the male guest is ignored rather than honoured, I ask if he is right. To call the male dancer a guest is to say that his role is secondary. Is it? If, for the moment, we consider only the ballerina and her male partner (while bearing in mind that at no time have they constituted the whole of ballet), then the answer is that in Petipa's 'baroque' time the male role was, indeed, secondary; so it was too, but by a much smaller margin, in the preceding romantic period. Giselle's Albrecht could not have been born later in the last century but even in the 1840s—and even by comparison with the role, no mean one, of James in *La Sylphide* (1832) —he seems to have been exceptional. And he is one of the main reasons why *Giselle* lives on so vigorously. But your Florimund and Siegfried of the baroque second half of the century are really no more than porters-in-chief, with a solo or two by way of tip. Since their time the balance has changed, but it has changed least in those ballets which are most classical. There the servitude of the male partner continues; it is much less rigorous than it was, there are occasions when the servile bonds have burst and perhaps it is a bit over the odds to call it a servitude any longer but, still, the ballerina does retain pride of place, the lioness's share. Nowadays Albrecht has been joined by many other exceptions to the rule; but the rule remains.

If, however, we increase the data, to include other roles in the classics besides that of ballerina's partner and to include other kinds of 20th century ballet besides those which are closest kin in technique, or in theme as well as technique, to the classics, then we get a rather different answer. I suppose it would be possible, but rather meaningless, to describe Dr Coppelius as secondary or as a guest— and similarly the Ugly Sisters, those outrageous pantomime dames, of Ashton's *Cinderella*, or Alain and Widow Simone (again a pantomime dame) of his *Fille mal gardée*; such obstreperous guests tend to steal the show. It seems to me that in character-roles, whether in the inherited classics or more in contemporary works which are close kin to them, the men have it over the women. If we then take the whole wide free-for-all of dramatic works, mainly or faintly classical or not classical at all, which make up the current repertory, we find that neither sex is really dominant; they share the limelight pretty evenly.

So Balanchine was right only over a limited and, I dare say dwindling area. Only fair to add that, stuck though he is with that women's lib remark of his, he has done quite a lot to gainsay it. The male contribution to his beautiful *Serenade* and his honourable *Concerto Barocco* is, admittedly, exiguous; but, for the rest, his disregard of the male guest is evident only in the less admirable of his classical exercises (*Symphony in C, Ballet Imperial, Allegro Brillante* etc.). Those busy, perfunctory, couplings of academic movement with 'absolute' music may be painfully numerous but against them can be set the celebrated *Agon* and one or two others of its kind, where the male-female balance is nearly even, also *Apollo* and *The Prodigal Son*—from the far off Diaghilevian days—where the male, surely, dominates. To pass from Balanchine to other 20th century examples: the male roles in Massine's ballets composed, many of the best of them, for himself, are certainly not secondary; in Ashton's purely classical *Symphonic Variations*, so often recurring *cum laude* in my text, the women are, albeit modestly, in the ascendant, but Ashton's *Dream* is decidedly Oberon's ballet rather than Titania's. The frowardness of the male guests in *La Fille* and *Cinderella* I have already mentioned. In Robbins's *Dances at a Gathering* (another much cited delight of mine) the balance is tilted neither way or, if anything, slightly in the men's favour—witness Nureyev, Dowell, Coleman in the Royal Ballet's performances. And no one who has seen Vassiliev and Liepa in *Spartacus*, the Bolshoi's signature ballet (so I regard it), could think they were secondary to their partners, even when one of those partners is Maximova.

The point which most obviously emerges from this short list of examples is that, even in the most classical of latter-day ballets, the man gets a much better showing than he did before; which is another way of repeating that Balanchine was only right to a small and decreasing extent. I confessed earlier to being generally less interested in male than in female dancing. That clearly is not, as it might well have been in the last century, because the male dancer is a humble fellow at the party, easy to overlook; he is that no longer. And if your enjoyment, like mine, of male dancers comes mainly not from demonstrations of pure or almost pure classicism but from more character-full performances, then you, like me, are still left nowadays with much male dancing to enjoy. Still the question remains: why, in my general predilection for female

dancers, do I find female classicism to be particularly satisfactory—
indeed, the very heart of the matter—whereas I am more lukewarm
about male classicism than about male character-roles? That question may be of more concern to me than to you but still I pursue it
in case I am not, as I believe I am not, quite singular in this. The
answer, I think, is that I ask for more intelligence, wit or what have
you from the men than from the women; technically accomplished
male gracefulness gives me comparatively little, whereas the female
counterpart gives me much. So it would seem that I pay the men
the doubtless unwelcome compliment of asking more from them.
So it would seem, too, that Balanchine and I become querulous
allies; allies because, if I read him right, he also gets less from male
dancing than from female, but querulous because he raises his
predisposition to a law whereas I regard mine as no more than a
personal bias, shared though it may be by some others. Anyway it
makes me, I dare say, the more thorough male chauvinist pig of
the two since he nowhere suggests that he asks less of the women
than of the men whereas I, by my own admission, ask just that. Be
that as it may it all, again, has everything to do with sex; and there
let it lie.

It is high time I said whom, apart from Massine, I have most
admired. Apart from Massine? Not quite yet. About him a little
more. His dancing had the tautness of a compressed spring; and a
snap and fingertip precision of movement and timing. It was virile,
not in any strutting, vainglorious way (what the Italians untrans-
latably call *gallismo*) but gallantly virile, or sternly, indignantly,
pathetically or, often, comically virile. Various though it was, it
bore the hall-mark of a constant, highly distinctive and intelligent
personality. He was, as I have said, slightly bow-legged; the tights
and abbreviated tunic of the *danseur noble* were not for him. (I
think I never saw him in a role which required them.) And, of
course, he was wonderfully well served by Massine the choreographer. Without his own choreography we would never have
known how great a dancer he could be; and that, oddly enough,
implies an adverse criticism not of his dancing but of his choreography.

Like all the world's bobby-soxers I have admired Nureyev though,
unlike theirs, my sometimes unwilling admiration has stopped well
short of screaming or swooning point. He has been devoted, not
without deviation, to the classics; or rather he has been their per-
emptory tyrant, for whenever an inherited version has left, or would

have left, him under-exercised he has added to the Prince's share of the proceedings; he so switched attention from Odette–Odile to Seigfried in his production of *Swan Lake* that some wag suggested its title should be changed to 'Siegfried's Dream', and in his production of *Beauty*, at least when he himself dances in it, poor Aurora becomes (almost) serving-girl to Florimund. On the face of it he might seem to breach my preference for male character-dancing over male classicism. But not so. Even when we first saw him in the west (in 1960) all shining new and brave with defection, there were other classicists who, judged by the academic rules, out-danced him; his Kirov colleague, Soloviev, was one of them. And when, to our lasting gratitude and by a feat of his extraordinary dance memory, he endowed the Royal Ballet with the Kirov's *Bayadère* (last act) I remember what a lumpy business he often made of Solor's leaping, turning solo, compared with the soaring neatness of the Royal Ballet's much less renowned Michael Coleman. Even at the top of his form, say ten years ago, he was no match for Baryshnikov or Vassiliev in breath-taking virtuosity. A classical virtuoso he certainly was, and is, but he has never been one to make it look debonair; his knottily muscled, unaristocratic physique proclaimed rather than concealed effort, and time, which has accentuated his muscles, has also accentuated this appearance of effort; he could, and still can, do much more than most but not, you feel, without trying damned hard. What, however, he had was stage-personality to the *n*th degree, a magnetism which was animal (pantherine), intelligent withal—and compulsive. The animal compulsiveness has dwindled —with familiarity perhaps—though not much; and the impression of intelligence in his dancing has more than correspondingly grown. The later Nureyev's stage-presence is certainly more subtle than the early one's, less blinkered in concentration on his own starriness, more concerned, whenever the role allows it, in character-interpretation; and (to me) this later Nureyev is the more compulsive one. But I am never quite sure how much my decreasingly reluctant admiration of his dancing is coloured by what I know of him as a more-than-dancer, an utterly devoted, intelligent and gifted disciple of the art of ballet. Perhaps he is not quite a choreographer; he himself insists that he is not, insists that the reason for the many 'Nureyev versions' of the classics, for so many companies, is that he wants to be sure of having a lot of dancing to do. It is true that his successes have been either in these adaptations of his or in ballets made entirely by other people, not in the few works which he has thought up *ab initio*. I used to believe that his singularly adult version of *The Nutcracker* was more than a derivative from Vaino-nen or Petipa–Ivanov or Ashton. But familiarity has persuaded me that even the *pas de deux* at the end of Act I, which is the most attractive dance sequence in the ballet, came like *La Bayadère* from his litmus paper memory rather than from true inventiveness. Still even that—such a capacity for the seamless interweaving of many and closely remembered scraps—would mark him as out of the ordinary. For all the egotistical, tyrannical, sometimes downright vulgar appearance of self-obsession which, though it has lessened, has not vanished, his strongest obsession is ballet not Nureyev. He is, in his own estimation, a disciple, a missionary, a prophet if you like, but not, appearances sometimes to the contrary, God. In his career, as in his dancing, he has shown a missionary's persistent courage; his career, at least until after 1960 and defection, was a brave and bitter victory over adversity and his dancing has never taken the easy option—always the grand test attempted, even if botched, rather than a face-saving evasion. In this I find the diff-erence between a true servant's pride and a watchful, self-centred exhibitionism; I find it endearing. When I see him dance I cannot quite escape, nor do I want to, from my gratitude: for the fillip he has given to public interest, particularly in male dancing—no one, since Nijinsky, has done so much for that—but also in ballet generally; for his missionary devotion to an art which he sometimes bullies but which, really, he ardently serves and for his obdurate courage. I have tried to make a distinction between dancers who 'do' and dancers who 'are'; Nureyev is something else again; not so much a super-star as a super-dynamo. All this tints my grateful vision when I see him take the stage, in his vulnerable, just slightly risible arrogance.

Nureyev, who does not easily praise other (male) dancers, has strenuously praised the Dane, Erik Bruhn. And rightly. Bruhn was not one of your simpering, classical princelings but a royal presence to be reckoned with; a combination of cool, unforced authority and impeccable precision. Our own Anthony Dowell is another arch-classicist whom I have greatly admired. He is, if anything, too fastidious; those solos which are the 'noble dancer's' rare oppor-tunity to dazzle—he will do them, or most of them, with supreme elegance but always, I feel, a little against the grain. Perhaps that is one reason why he became so popular; rare, and nice, to find anyone so good at it who dislikes showing off. His Oberon in Ashton's

Dream is another matter; a 'show-off' role, and the dominant one in this beautiful ballet, but made for him and tailored exactly to his pyrotechnical elegance, to his reticent dignity and to his ability to turn like an unemotional top. An even better role for him is Mowgli, 'the boy with matted hair', in Tudor's *Shadowplay* or, if not 'better', then more astonishing because it adapts his singularly pure classicism to such mysteriously dramatic ends. He made his name as Antoinette Sibley's partner; but it was during her absence, on 'maternity leave', that his dancing—with other partners or with none—grew to greatness. Already he was the prize male product of the British classical school; in his new independence he became the Royal Ballet's most authoritative dancer, of either sex—and that in a company which had always been chiefly honoured, not only by me, for its ballerinas.

Woizikowsky and Shabelevsky are two I remember as brilliant character dancers of de Basil's time; the one a survivor from the Diaghilev company, the other quite new to us in the 1930s. Michael Somes, for so long Fonteyn's eminently reliable and dignified partner, was not eminent as a *danseur noble*—a true but too broad-beamed prince—but he was, and is, more musical both naturally and by study than any of them, male or female: an example of exceptional musicality unallied with a physical aptitude for comparably musical movement. With his timing and his dramatic sense he has, however, become that rarity of western ballet, a fine, senior character-actor (rather than dancer). For me at least, his vignette of Armand's father in *Marguerite and Armand*, which Ashton made so explicitly for the autumnal Fonteyn and the young Nureyev, is more memorable than anything achieved therein by the two stars. What, I wonder, happened to Yevdokimov who, on the Bolshoi's first visit to Covent Garden, turned the brief solo and coda of the peasant *pas de deux* (*Giselle*) into something unforgettable: classical pyrotechnics made to seem effortless. The Bolshoi's Vassiliev, whose extraordinary, tireless leaps and turns are the great compensation for the vulgarities of *Spartacus*—I, like everyone else, have been quite stunned by him; but when I recover from his almost literally breath-taking impact I realize he is no sort of actor; highly trained vigour personified but not the kind of male dancing which has meant most to me.

When I first saw the American Ballet Theatre nearly 30 years ago it was the three men, and especially the dynamic John Kriza, in *Fancy Free* who impressed me most of all. That exuberant, jazzy, athletic vitality, not easily confinable in the duties and dignities of a *danseur noble*, then seemed very American—the characteristic, distinctive contribution of the American male ballet dancer. I found it much more exhilarating than the polite, pallid manners of (for instance) the contemporary Sadler's Wells male classicist. I think that since then, perhaps because the best American ballet has gone more classical, this distinctiveness has somewhat dwindled—though there is still a marvellous robustness about the (classical) virtuosity of Edward Villella. Villella, a mighty dancer, has, for some years now, been the acknowledged prince of the NYCB and, indeed, of American ballet generally. There have been other male dancers of much distinction, the negro Arthur Mitchell, founder of the Harlem Dance Theatre, prominent among them. Nor would I dare to omit here a reference to the Royal Danish Ballet, which produced the great Erik Bruhn, has consistently continued to produce fine male dancers and has, just as consistently, lost them to foreign companies; Egon Madsen, for instance, to Stuttgart, and Peter Martins to the NYCB.

So I come to the one man who, quite recently, has rivalled, if not ousted, Massine as my favourite. Predictably, perhaps, he is an American, but belongs to European ballet; he is the Stuttgart Company's Richard Cragun. I do not have life-enhancing memories of him, as I do of Massine, in half a dozen roles and over a spread of performances through several years. No, my delight rests on a performance or two in just one role, that of Petrucchio, in Cranko's *Taming of the Shrew*. Not that he has lacked distinction in the other ballets (nearly all of them, I think, Cranko—or Balanchine—classical) in which I have seen him; in them he has—no small honour—put me in mind of Nureyev's uncopied model, Erik Bruhn: the same sort of clean-cut linear effect and an easy, laconic authority which is an American cousin of Bruhn's rather older-style but still lightly worn Danish princeliness. But as Petrucchio he has much more than that; he co-ordinates the uttermost in classical 'show-off' with a sense of character rarely found in any performance and never, in my experience, in one which depends so much on academic technique. The result is swashbuckling, almost Rabelaisian, extraordinarily authoritative; and it is funnier than anything else I have seen in ballet; a joy to eye and mind—and temper. To rate him so high on the strength of just one role might, I suppose, seem disproportionate. No matter. To have combined, even once, such dancing with such acting is, in my league table, to have transcended them all. The Katharine, by the way, to his Petrucchio is Marcia Haydée, who is his partner off the stage as well as on it. A partnership as right as right could be.

Richard Cragun has delighted me in one whole, big role; Haydée has also delighted me throughout entire roles and by her variety. Yet the keenest pleasure given me by my favourite dancers and which has sometimes sufficed to make them my favourites, has come not mainly from the large-scale interpretations but from the little things, the brief episodes or, even more, the snapshots (as it were) of a movement or posture which have stuck in my memory as an anthology of consolations for bad nights or rainy days; and in this I doubt if I am singular. A few of these I have mentioned on the way: Sibley's delicately eloquent feet in the Dorabella variation of *Enigma*; Penney elegantly up-ended in *Song of the Earth*; the click of Massine's heels before he began to court Riabouchinska in *Beau Danube*; Dowell aloof, top-like, circling and circling in the *scherzo* of *The Dream*. To them I add: Fonteyn fascinated by her shadow and dancing with it in *Ondine* (this, for me, has been the little signature dance of all her long career); Fonteyn again just standing, feet crossed, down stage, left, in *Symphonic Variations*; Massine again in *Beau Danube*, with raised arms and fluttering hands, protesting against the street dancer's (justified) vilification; Baronova with tambourine, on point, as she 'bourrée-ed' towards us in *Le Coq d'Or*; Makarova's incredibly controlled slow turns in the lake-side *pas de deux* of *Swan Lake*; Maximova, all glitter, precision and provocation in the *Don Q pas de deux*; Seymour's shy, perilous overtures to the elder man in *The Invitation*; Carolyn Adams prancing, gently, musically across stage in Paul Taylor's *Aureole* (otherwise a forgettable work); June Highwood, a young, inconspicuous Royal Ballet girl, turning the repetitive undulations of Christopher Bruce's unimportant choreography in *Unfamiliar Playground* into sudden sensual magic; and Merle Park at hurricane speed in the 'autumn variation' of Ashton's *Cinderella* or, as Juliet in MacMillan's ballet, running down the stairs from her balcony to meet her Romeo—there was never another dancer, not even Ulanova, who could run, with such fleet, stylized naturalness, as she can.

The ballerinas, past, present and incipient, have given me most of these memories. But their partners have, evidently, contributed. I have, I think, shown that my myopia is not complete. Besides, however true or untrue may be Balanchine's contention that it is a woman's world, it is also, and much less disputably, the world of

Ashton, Robbins, MacMillan, Fokine, Massine, Petipa, Ivanov and Balanchine himself. The women are there as well among the choreographers, but vastly out-gunned and out-numbered. And it is the choreographers who are hosts to the dancers and to us.

SIX

Things to come

Maurice Béjart, who is important but whom I have not mentioned before, says he wants to bring ballet to the masses. He does it too. His Ballet of the Twentieth Century is extraordinary in possessing three home-grounds, in or near Brussels, where this Marseillais choreographer-manager, one-time dancer, shows the Belgians their first ever national ballet company in action. Béjart would be displeased to have his company described as 'national'; he is all for the universality of his balletic message and, while recognizing that other companies may properly and laudably fly a national flag, it is not one he wants to fight under. Still, there he and his company are, accommodated and cherished by the Bruxellois in the Théâtre de la Monnaie, which is conventional middle-sized, and in the Cirque Royale and the Forêt Nationale, which are vast. The only time I have seen the company on a home-ground was in the arena of the Cirque Royale where it was showing the Béjart–Berlioz *Romeo and Juliet*. From that performance I chiefly remember—I shall not easily forget—some two-score couples grappling and undulating on the ground, what time a loudspeaker proclaimed over Berlioz's most lyrical music; 'Don't make war, make love'. Such is Béjart. He has done much better than that desecration of Berlioz (which enraptured the Belgian audience) and though some people find his choreography mostly ghastly a great many more, including me, do not. We are the lowbrows, with a sprinkling, perhaps, of the *very* highbrows; and Béjart is after us. He succeeds with us here in Europe, where the critics have mixed views about him; more amusingly he succeeds also in the U.S. and, specifically, in New York where the critics have all damned him beyond, you might think, redemption; only to be answered by the stampede of the young of Manhattan to see him in Brooklyn. I have not mentioned him before because he is not a good choreographer in any sense that would have been relevant to my arguments; he is not inventive of steps and there is really nothing in 'the Béjart manner' which is not derivative. You would recognize a Béjart ballet not by any stylistic signature but, very likely, by its size, by the grandiloquence of its pretensions, (if you happened to read the always copious programme notes) and, not seldom, by the assault it makes on great music.

Or you might recognize it, more favourably, by its theatrical flair. This Béjart has abundantly; better than almost any other dance-producer or choreographer he knows what works in the theatre and how to make it do so. One reason why he is important is that he applies this theatrical flair to the large, simplified effects which tell in stadiums; he has not so much a sense of the theatre, though that too, as of the stadium or arena. He brings ballet to the masses, 20,000 at a time.

That the European and North American reactions to him are somewhat dissimilar—popular enthusiasm on both continents but much more unanimous damnation by the critics over there—is a separate and irrelevant point. Still I venture an explanation: American dance criticism is wonderfully serious minded, and is outraged by the obvious nonsense of Béjart's intellectual pretensions, whereas over here that rubbish is brushed aside (nor, I think is Béjart himself more than quarter-fooled by it). It is not that the American critics are less gullible; they take seriously a whole lot of home-grown American 'jabberwocky', Twyla Tharp's for instance, or Meredith Monk's, which is much less esteemed over here. They resent Béjart because his blatant absurdities blow the gaff on the pretensions which proliferate about the American dance scene; they resent him because they are too sophisticated to lie back and enjoy his theatrical flair, as the uninhibited young do, and not sophisticated enough to see that his bogusness is the least of him. Or so it seems to me.

Béjart is also important because, some think, he points to a future when ballet, if it is not to be killed by costs, will have to make a habit of the Béjart speciality. The time is coming, so the argument runs, when ballet will no longer be able to expect subvention by national or local government or by the (mostly American) 'foundations', which enables expensive programmes to be presented to audiences of 1,500 to 2,000—the more or less typical opera house's capacity. A division will have to come between really large-scale, stadium sized, financially viable ballet and inexpensive 'chamber', or small theatre ballet, which will, no doubt, need more than the box-office's support but will not cost a great deal.

If this is the prospect before us it will mean the end of things as we have known them. For, Béjart apart, ballet is not geared to a stadium sized operation and cannot be without sacrificing its best. The biggest productions for an opera house are, I suppose, those of the classics, though, by Béjart standards, they are only middle-sized. They require a wealth and variety of scenery which cannot be managed in a stadium; and, more important, their choreography is full of delicacies which, in a large arena, become scarcely discernible, if discernible at all. Yes, an approximation can be, and has been, so presented, but not without artistic loss which may be acceptable occasionally but would be unacceptable if such presentations were to become the rule. If the 19th century 'spectaculars' cannot stand this treatment nor can the more intimate, but still middle-sized 20th century 'classics' such as *Symphonic Variations* and *Dances at a Gathering*; these, and many others, may be relatively adaptable because they need less scenery but the loss in the observable nuances of their choreography is even greater. The Hollywood Bowl, for instance, is all very well once in a while for a blurred, distant view of *Les Sylphides*, as I found when I saw the Royal Ballet perform in that large amphitheatre. Those far-off patterns of animated tulle had a charm of their own. But as a standard presentation of this delicate, detailed choreography it would have been intolerable. Choreography for stadiums, if that became the rule, would have to be simpler, broader, more circus-like, a blunter instrument.

I do not see, however, that ballet need go, mainly, that way, or is likely to. True that at a time of financial stress governments and 'foundations' may blink a bit at the cost of supporting a national or civic ballet, especially when it is linked with the still more expensive maintenance of opera. The wind of official favour blows now warmer, now colder; and at the moment of my writing it is blowing colder than at any time in the past quarter century. Cold enough to suggest that during the remainder of this century there is unlikely to be a further proliferation of ballet companies, at least in Europe and America, comparable with that, especially in the U.S. and Western Germany, of the years since the war. But never so cold, by my guess, as to reverse the trend in western Europe and North America (Australia too) towards official and semi-official subvention of the arts, and of this art in particular. A consolidation—which always implies some retrenchment—rather than a change of attitude: that is what we can expect.

It is worth looking, with an eye to the guessable future, a bit more closely at the situations in the U.S. and the German Federal Republic. There, as I have said, ballet's recent expansion has been greatest. Inevitably, not all this wide and rapid growth is solid. Some of it is decidedly rickety.

Every German region or State or *Land* has, long since, had its own opera house; that is a legacy of the time when there was not one Germany but a host of separate German kingdoms, principalities and archdukedoms; of course, it is also a tribute to the German passion for music. Since the war two relevant things have happened; the one, a result of the belated and strenuous fear engendered by Hitler's strongly centralized Germany, is that in the new Federal Republic a lot of responsibility has devolved on the States or *Laende*, including the responsibility for the arts. The other development is that, in Germany, ballet—and I mean classical rather than modern type dance—has at last caught on; *das Land ohne Ballett* now has almost as many dance companies as it has opera companies and opera houses and I have, personally, only come across one of them, that of Cologne, which goes in for 'contemporary' dance rather than ballet. (Darmstadt was, I believe, the only other exception.) Because no restriction of nationality is put on the employment of dancers by these companies—as it is by the Royal Ballet, to which only British or Commonwealth citizens may belong—the Federal Republic has become the greatest and most open of dancers' markets; a godsend to the annual hordes of young hopefuls who tumble out of the ballet schools of (particularly) the U.S. and Britain. Each year, for instance, the Royal Ballet School produces 25 or more graduates of whom, say, ten are accepted into the Royal Ballet itself; many of the remainder go to Germany. One vivid example of the voraciousness of the German demand, and of the ample supply of dancers to meet it, came my way in 1974 when the Frankfurt ballet had a brief season in Birmingham. This was only two years after all but half a dozen of its members had departed with the previous artistic director (the American, John Neumeier) to Hamburg. Yet there they were in Birmingham, nearly all of them brand new members and under a new director; and an excellent, if not very integrated, international company they were.

The German market is, as I say, big and open. But I wonder how long it will so continue. So far only one of the many new or newish companies has been built to last—supported, that is, by a school of its own. That one is Stuttgart's, the joint achievement of John Cranko and his exceptionally helpful Intendant, Dr E Schaefer. Only Stuttgart has made a long-term commitment. So far its company has been as international as the rest of them with its South African, Royal Ballet-trained, director (now succeeded by the American, Glen Tetley), its Brazilian *assoluta*, Haydée, and its American leading male dancer, Cragun—not to speak of the Danish Egon Madsen and other foreigners as well as, admittedly, the two Germans, Birgit Keill and Hans Klaus. The school has not yet had time to turn pupils into professionals: but soon it will do so and the result is bound to be that the Stuttgart Ballet will become much more German, much less open to dancers from abroad. 'Bad luck on the foreign aspirants but, to my mind, good that ballet should be rooted in its locality, whether national or regional. That way it is likely to be more various and to express national or local style and talent rather than to be an international, anonymous hotchpotch. Not that I foresee a collapse of all those other West German groups which have not matched Stuttgart's long-term investment. For the foreseeable future there will certainly be no lack of foreign-trained dancers to fill their ranks. But they are rickety. The enthusiasm which, in a time of growing national wealth, expanded those humble, long established groups, the 'Opera Ballet', only required for the dance sequences in grand opera, and turned them into veritable companies with their *Ballett Abende* at the Opera House, could easily evaporate when times are hard, as they are at present (albeit less so in Germany than elsewhere).

It is more likely, to my mind, that in ten years from now the number of worthwhile ballet companies in the opera houses of the Federal Republic will be fewer by, perhaps, half a dozen, than that any of them will have followed Stuttgart's example and invested in the long, reliable and expensive future which is implied by a school. But that would still leave the Federal Republic's development of state-supported ballet as a remarkable one, more widely disseminated than in any other west European nation and outdone in quality, possibly but not certainly, by the Royal Ballet alone.

In the U.S. dance companies come for a brief summer; a chill winter kills them. Every choreographer everywhere wants his own company but only in that nation of affluence and free enterprise can almost any choreographer find someone to back him, along with a group of his own. The 'foundations' have also helped; so, latterly, have the home town, the state and the federal government. Even in the U.S. private support for dance, as for the other arts, has been increasingly supplemented, if not replaced, by official or quasi-official funds. But as the support is brisk and widespread, so also is it mercurial and short-winded. The companies come and go. An Eliot Feld quickly makes his name as a choreographer, soon acquires his own company and soon disbands it. Occasionally a choreo-grapher-manager survives an adverse change in his backer's fancy. Robert Joffrey was not to be done down by the withdrawal of the Harkness money; he went, and has continued to go, his own way, with a re-formed and considerable company though not without a lot of new financial difficulties which have recently threatened to overwhelm him. Meanwhile Rebekah Harkness, having fallen out with Joffrey, set up her own company, even endowed it with its very own New York theatre in 1974 and then, within a few months of that lavish gesture, announced that the company would be no more. Mercurial and arbitrary indeed. In all that large, and still extraordinarily rich country where almost every city contains earnest organizations, professional, semi-professional or wholly amateur, for the promotion of ballet and other forms of theatrical dance, there are, I would say, two institutions which, by virtue of longevity and accomplishment, qualify as durable, top class: the New York City Ballet and American Ballet Theatre. I would guess that these two will continue; but my bet, especially on Ballet Theatre, would not be a big one. Sentiment almost teases me into mentioning the Martha Graham Company as another likely stayer. The time, how-ever, has long since come when that dynamic lady's importance is no longer, or scarcely, to be found in the company which bears her name and which, nowadays, is so seldom brought together for performances. Not her group but her world-wide influence matters now. The splendidly appointed Graham school in New York will surely persist; so will the Graham doctrine, though with more and more glosses on it by her disciples and her disciples-turned-rebel. And that, at least on the evidence of the one occasion when she spoke to me about her septuagenarian ambitions, is how she would want it to be; she wants her monument to be not so much her company or her choreography as the spirit of the Graham philosophy.

The New York City Ballet, oldest of the American companies, dates back traceably, though not by name, to the meeting between Lincoln Kirstein and Balanchine in London in 1933. First and last it has meant Balanchine, as choreographer and presiding genius. Nowadays it is trying to mean Jerome Robbins as well and, generally, to be less dependent on the fertility of just one choreographer. Not that Balanchine, in his seventies, is an extinct volcano; his genius re-re-re-erupted in a profusion of new ballets for the obsequies of Stravinsky in 1973. In any case, the repertory which he has provided down the years, even when all that was hurried, perfunctory, ephemeral in it has been discounted, is a treasure-store on which a company could expect to live for quite a while. Yet continued eminence, if not survival for another decade or two, will depend on the company's success in broadening its choreographic base. So far, apart from what Robbins has done for it, efforts to this end have not been fruitful. I cannot, however, see it going under; nor can I see it remaining quite so distinctive or distinguished as it has been, not because I undervalue Robbins's talent, which, in its more eclectic way, is as remarkable as Balanchine's (perhaps more so), but because Robbins is less prolific and has never been so single-minded in his devotion. The solution, mooted from time to time, and now more urgently, might well be a Joffrey–NYCB amalgamation; Robert Joffrey, not the greatest of choreographers, has certainly proved himself an imperturable master in management.

The NYCB has had its financial worries—it has them now—but nothing to compare with those of Ballet Theatre. This, the second oldest company in the U.S., has seldom been far from extinction since it began in 1940 and always it has come through. My guess is that its expertise in survival, its acrobatic brinkmanship, will continue to save it—that reinforced by its remarkable repertory. Like but unlike the NYCB it has become a valuable choreographic museum, the difference being that, whereas the NYCB is where you go to see Balanchine, Ballet Theatre is a showcase for all-sorts. The choreographer who has come closest to stamping it with his personality is Antony Tudor; and it is still the only company to have the right to present *Pillar of Fire* and the Tudor *Romeo and Juliet*. But it has been essentially, and has increasingly become, an unspecialized museum, reflecting a variety of tastes and owing allegiance to no one god except, erratically, the god of classicism. Which is another way of saying that it lives by the star-system—by, for instance, snapping up such celebrated defectors as Makarova and Barishnikov. Latterly it has perhaps over-reached itself; a super-abundance of stars can be almost as embarrassing as a lack of them. Not a model for aspiring company managers to emulate, but a hardy exception—very hard to kill.

If this implies that even the brightest luminaries of the American firmament are fragile, their future a flickering uncertainty, that is just what I mean to imply. But that is not to suggest a drear prospect for American ballet and, generally, for American dance. On the one hand there is this insecurity at the top; on the other there is a vitality of 'dance activity'—a vitality at the grassroots—from East Coast to West. Professional companies may come and go; today's new princeling of choreography may be dethroned tomorrow, but there are always more choreographers and companies to follow; and there are the amateur organizations galore. The insecurity at the top could well be seen not as a frailty but as a result of the casualness that goes with an awareness of cornucopian reserves. It is true that, as I have said, the NYCB has so far had scant success in discovering the sort of choreographer who might supplement, and eventually succeed, Jerome Robbins in taking over from Balanchine (how could anyone quite 'take over' from that ageless dynamo?); true also that the American scene, like the world-wide one, shows a superabundance of dance-groups in pursuit of a scanty number of choreographers. Yet the home and, I would say emphatically, the hope of new choreography are now in the U.S. rather than anywhere else. Worthwhile choreographers may be too few to go round, even in the U.S. to say nothing of the rest of the world, but it is there that most of these rarities are now and, I believe, will continue to be found. There, it seems to me the creative spirit of dance is most fecund.

Out of this fecundity I do not expect another great choreographer to emerge in the foreseeable future. Greatness, you may say, is never to be expected; it always comes as a surprise. True enough; nevertheless, it does cast its shadow before it and, to me at least, no such shadow is now visible. I expect that to happen in ballet which has long since happened in modern dance; as, after Graham, there has been a splintering of 'contemporary' creative talent, so, after the line of greatness from Fokine to Robbins, there will be, for the long time being, a lot of little ballet-makers. Let time disprove me.

I once asked Balanchine what he thought about the shortage of young or youngish choreographers. Where were his successors? He, characteristically, made light of it; really good choreographers had always been very scarce; in the grand days of Tsarist ballet, for instance, there had been only one (Petipa) or at most two (Ivanov being added as an afterthought). One had been quite enough then, one was all that could be expected now and, in due course, another would turn up. This was Balanchine having his bit of fun, pretending to live down to his reputation for blinkered arrogance. In fact, ballet in this century has, so far, been rich in choreographers beyond the dreams of any previous period. Agreed, for the sake of avoiding unhelpful argument, that one or two sufficed for 50 years of the Maryinsky, but that is not to say that the greatly increased number in this century is enough, much less excessive, for the demands of a world of ballet which now spreads from Stockholm to Cape Town, from Edinburgh to Auckland.

Maurice Béjart has said that as the 19th was the century of opera so the 20th is that of ballet. I think he is right. But it is possible now to be more specific. The first two-thirds of the century (more or less) has been ballet's great period of creativeness; the remaining third will, by my guess, be a time of conservation—there being more to conserve than was ever worth conserving before and, thanks to dance notation, more hope of conserving it. Not only this or that company but the whole world of ballet is becoming a museum; one in which pride of place goes to the few and precious surviving exhibits from the last century—the works of Balanchine's 'one or two'. But these by now take up a relatively declining, though still most important, share of the expanding show-space. The rest goes to the achievements of the 20 Diaghilevian years and of the many great choreographers who have come up since that time. The Diaghilevian galaxy of choreographers was, indeed, brilliant: Fokine, Nijinsky, Massine, Nijinska and the young Balanchine— and what a difference they have made to the subsequent international repertory. Their successors have been, perhaps, less revolutionary—but, for memorable choreography, revolutionary or not, the older Balanchine (I count him twice—and why not?), Ashton, Tudor, Robbins, and Cranko and MacMillan too, have surely matched and even surpassed the Diaghilevian achievements. The conservation of ballets is, as I have tried to show in an earlier chapter, a rum business—more often than not a conservation of music but any amount of re-jigging or renovation or even total displacement of the choreography, not least in the revered classics; and it may well be that much of the most honoured post-Diaghilevian choreography, still too recent to be subjected to major change, will go through many vicissitudes in the course of its 'conservation'. The fact remains that the international repertory is enormously indebted to these choreographers, the great ones of Diaghilev's régime and after. All of them, except Fokine, Nijinsky and Cranko are still alive (Cranko's death being sadly premature) and they may yet astonish us with new, memorable productivity; but, truth to tell, none of them, with the exception of Robbins who is now one of the most senior, seems likely to do so. And where are their successors? Minor, younger figures, yes—these abound; and, as I have said, the main hope now lies in the changeful, impatient vitality of the U.S. But the signs of incipient greatness are not there.

So we are in for a time of conservation. And if, even now or now even more than before, this, and the last century's conservable output is not enough to supply the many companies of ballet's expanded world with separate, distinctive repertories, it can, nevertheless, provide enough to make a programme basis. Yet I do not at all suggest that conservation implies or will imply satisfaction with things as they are. Ballet, in this century, has been ever hungry for novelty; modern dance is hungrier still. Even the classics are altered time and again and even a relatively unexperimental company, such as the Royal Ballet is now considered to be, is likely to put on two or three new works in a year. Ballet's turnover is rapid, its wastage large, and in modern dance the speed of turnover is almost frenzied, the wastage enormous. One reason, of course, why ballet's much reproduced classics are so often altered is that, compared with the standard works of opera, there are so few of them; and a reason why ballet's turnover is so rapid is that a ballet, compared with an opera, is, as a rule, inexpensive to produce; and, again, modern dance is inexpensive when compared with ballet. These things are not going to change. In the coming time of conservation the hunger for novelty will not decrease, nor will the turnover of new or new-fangled productions get any less rapid. If change there is, it is likely to be that the turnover will, in fact, accelerate—and never mind dance notation's preservative power: because the up-and-coming choreographers are as numerous as they are unremarkable and interchangeable—when compared with their mighty predecessors. When a company has Balanchine, Ashton or Robbins on its pay-roll, there is no need to go hunting choreography in the back streets.

Take away the giants and the search becomes wide, the preferences become ephemeral.

That said, my guess is not that, along with the conservation of the great past, there will be a mere chaos of minor, new choreography. There will, of course, be some pattern to it. In chapter 3 I noted two tendencies in the copious choreography of this century so far; the one towards a widening of the frontiers, to take in all sorts of styles and themes, the other towards developing (rarifying, you might say) the classical idiom itself. Both tendencies will continue, hard though it may be at present to see how the frontiers can well be widened any further. I think—and this, to some extent, covers both tendencies—choreography's future belongs, mainly but not solely, to the eclectics; to such as van Manen who has produced works which are classical with modern trimmings (or, in his *Four Schumann Pieces*, almost entirely without them) for the Royal Ballet and the Dutch National Company, as well as far-fetched extravagances for the 'progressive' Netherlands Dance Theatre; or to one like Glen Tetley, the American, who made his name in Britain by his modernist work for the Ballet Rambert, gave the Royal Ballet its first two wholly unclassical productions (*Field Figures* and *Laborinthus*) and yet made, subsequently, the largely classical and beautiful *Gemini* for the Australian Ballet and the equally impressive and classical *Voluntaries* for the Stuttgart Company—of which company, symptomatically, he has now become the head, in succession to the Royal Ballet's classically trained John Cranko. And among these eclectics Jerome Robbins is the prince and the tall signpost: almost all classical in what he has done for the Royal Ballet and in most of what he has done for the NYCB but also the maker of *West Side Story* and much else that is jazzy or Grahamesque and not classical at all. The future largely belongs to the van Manens, the Tetleys and the after-Robbinses. Accordingly it also belongs to the companies which are variously skilled enough to carry out these eclectics' intentions; and that (harking back to what I said in chapter 2) means that it belongs to the classically trained. Only they can cope, as the Royal Ballet has already had to, with Tetley and van Manen as well as with Petipa, Balanchine and Ashton. They will have to cope with much more 'way out' idioms in the years to come. (Not that 'way out' is a synonym for 'technically difficult'. Decidedly the contrary.)

But to say that the future of choreography belongs mainly to the eclectics does not mean that every new ballet will be eclectic in style. The pointer is there, in the continuing popularity of the 19th century classics; they stand out, increasingly, as the indestructibles amid a proliferation of ephemera. The 20th century ballets which are likely to vie with them in staying power are those which are also most classical; examples not of pastiche but of the refinement of the tradition to an even purer essence; examples, in fact, of one of the century's two main choreographic tendencies. This, indeed, has to be qualified by what was said in chapter 4—that the durability even of the best choreography is imperilled when that choreography is tied to the best, most self-sufficient music. Nevertheless it is the neo-classical ballets of Ashton, Robbins, Balanchine, which are most likely to survive from our times. And if those, then also the works of any other of their successors who, however eclectic they may be, will still give their main allegiance (and whole ballets) to classicism. Minor and principally American successors they may be (by my guess), but for them too this will be the way to make, as some of them will, works which last. The rest—everything, if you like, which is implied by an attempt to widen the frontiers—will be the ephemera; and of them there will be a lot.

I have made my guesses about the future of ballet in the U.S. and West Germany. Time to say something about the prospect in Britain; which means the prospect for the Royal Ballet. If, in the matter of choreography, ballet generally has had it rich and good during this century, no company has had it quite so rich in home-grown talent as our national one for the past 40 years or so; Ashton, Cranko, MacMillan, Howard, de Valois and, latterly, Tudor—they make quite a list. Too much to expect that such wealth could be indefinitely renewed, and the signs are that for the time being it will not be. That is sad; we cannot but regret the passing of British choreographic productivity and pre-eminence. On the other hand, in a time of conservation the Royal Ballet will be particularly well placed. Unlike the NYCB it is a museum, not of one artist (who may not always be quite so fashionable as he is now) but of many. Like the American Ballet Theatre its collection is wide-ranging but it is much more comprehensive, as ballet-history, and much less haphazard. It is the richest museum of them all. Its dancers are, correspondingly, the most versatile and authoritative. If the future belongs to the dancers and companies who are adaptable enough to cope with the choreographic eclectics, then here are those who will cope best; and not only with whatever the eclectics may turn out but with the whole range of choreography back to and, of course, including Petipa and Ivanov. What it comes to is that the Royal Ballet has done singularly well in maintaining its basic, classical standards, while, recently at least, giving room to 'contemporary' influences (if not to the wildest of them).

In our preferences we are all tied to our period. My rather long 'Royal' period has been from Fonteyn, Shearer, Helpmann to Sibley, Park, Seymour, Dowell; and I admit to old fogeyish difficulty in rating the latest roses in the Garden as quite so beautiful or, at least, so stimulating as those of the last quarter century. I admit to no such, or much less, vulnerability of judgement about choreography, that more rationally judgeable entity; but about the performers, bearing in mind what was said in chapter 5 about the idiosyncracies of our judgements of members of the other sex on stage (or off it), I do admit that time, which hardens the arteries of other people's taste, may even have hardened mine. Nevertheless, even an old fogey can see that when the 'Royal' *corps de ballet* was honoured, as it was only last year, as the top star of British ballet in 1974, this amounts to a just recognition that the Royal Ballet is managing to stay exceptionally strong where strength matters most for the company's future—that is, in the quality of its rank and file. And, with whatever old fogeyish reluctance, I have come to realize that the young, technically iron-clad, yet also lyrical, Lesley Collier (whom I here mention for the first time) has improved so much of late that give her another year and she may vie with, almost, the best of my memories. If Collier then, very likely, others with her or soon after her, and others after them. If the signs are that Royal Ballet choreography is in for a slump, then the signs are also that the standard of Royal Ballet dancing is not. Having lavished praise on Soviet dancers, as distinct from Soviet choreography, earlier in this book, I found in the summer of 1974, when the Bolshoi again visited London, that the dead hand of Soviet taste seemed at last to have touched, and withered, Soviet dance standards (about that more in the Appendix). I fear no comparable infection of the Royal Ballet's dance standards, even in a museum period of choreography; for here, in America too, the conditions are conspicuously different and healthier.

Of course I could be entirely wrong. Instead of the time of conservation and consolidation which I foresee, there may (for instance) be remarkable developments in televised dance—about which I have said nothing at all—so that dance on TV becomes as significant a supplement to dance on stage as film acting has been to stage

acting. There have, indeed, been many successful 'ballets' on the
TV and cinema screens but, so far, they have been the work,
almost wholly, of the cartoonists. How to marry the choreography of
human dance, as distinct from the wonderful, infinitely fantastic
cavortings of cartoon-creatures, to the real and separate choreography of the camera and cutting-room—that is something which
producers/directors have scarcely begun to learn. Or a stupendous
new stage choreography may arise, sooner rather than later, in
America or, more improbably, in Europe. I would bet against it
but would be glad to be wrong.

Besides, there are even now areas of the world where ballet has
only half-conquered, if conquered at all. And if, as I said in my
first chapter, it remains finally mysterious why this migratory art,
received enthusiastically almost wherever it appears, puts down
roots now here, now there, then the possibility is not to be ruled out
that the present, worthy (national or regional) balletic enterprise of,
say, Canada may become even more important than the multitudinous balletic activities of the U.S.; or the Australian Ballet, an
up-and-coming youngster, even more closely indebted than the
Canadian one to British parentage may, sooner or later, outdo the
Royal Ballet itself. There is ballet in South America and South
Africa, and much enthusiasm for it. There is also ballet in China;
in Tokyo eight companies, no less, are now doing nicely. As it
happens, we have recently seen in London the first Japanese ballerina to take the lead in a British company's production of that
most un-Japanese classic, *Coppelia*; she did it with charming aplomb.
As I write these words the Tokyo Ballet, armed with a western
classical repertory, is expected in a month or so at Sadler's Wells,
that foundation theatre of British ballet. And as a coincidental prelude to that visitation I shall, in the meantime, have been in Japan
getting my first glimpse of Nipponese ballet on its home-ground.
So, who knows? I may find in Tokyo or Osaka or Yokohama the
next centre, or the next but one or two, of ballet's world. Perhaps I
think it unlikely that the oriental flowering of so western an art
could quite rival, still less dwarf, the western products. But what
with the present and, surely continuing shortage of choreographers
and with the opportunities for international exchange which exist
now as never before, there is going to be a mighty lot of cross-fert-
ilization. So, who knows?

Appendix

When the Bolshoi Ballet visited London in the summer of 1974, the evidence it provided about the state of that most famous company was discouraging. This I have mentioned in the final chapter. I did not think it quite reason enough for changing the more laudatory comments on Soviet ballet made earlier in the book. Leave it to time, I thought, to sort that one out. But it seemed worthwhile to reprint, to stand on its own, the following article of mine which appeared in *The Dancing Times* of August 1974.

What went wrong with the Bolshoi 1974?

This is an attempt to sum up the 'Bolshoi 1974', based on the evidence of that most famous company's fourth visit to London (at the Coliseum, June 12–July 20). As my conclusions, right or wrong, are scarcely favourable it is, I think, all the more prudent to begin by saying just what evidence I collected. I saw the whole repertory— the two veritable classics, *Swan Lake* and *Giselle*, the two more questionable classics, *Don Quixote* and *The Nutcracker*, and the Bolshoi's very own, inimitable *Spartacus*. I saw changes of cast in all of them except 'Don Q'—nine performances in all; and I saw all the more prominent principals except Vladimirov who was off for much of the season. But I doubt if he or, for that matter, Plisetskaja and the other seniors who were touring Canada and the U.S., at the time—in a large Bolshoi–Kirov concert group, including Barishnikov, of the Kirov, who defected during the tour—would have made all that difference to my over-all view; Plisetskaja, after all, we have seen here before when she was five years younger.

It would be hard to say which of the two veritable classics was the sadder. The *Swan Lake* was Yuri Grigorovich's production which had been just too late to get into the company's repertory for its third visit to London, in 1969. It was sad because all its many choreographic deviations from the more conventional version, or versions, were for the worse, except, arguably, the shortened, dramatically concentrated final act; it gave a deplorable impression of Bolshoi-sponsored 'improvements' to the classics. The intention was evidently to make it more Siegfried's ballet and less Odette-Odile's. That explains why Act I began with the Prince dancing to music suitable not to a solo but to an entry of courtiers, and why, again, the Prince partnered the two soloists in a jejune version of the (first act) pas-de-trois. But it does not explain why the national dances of Act III were bereft of all character and turned into a series of feeble, almost undifferentiated exercises on pointe—precisely what Petipa did not do and what Fokine buried 70 years ago. *Giselle* was sad rather differently; for here was recognizably the production in which Ulanova, supported by excellent soloists and a flawless corps de ballet, had so impressed us in 1956, when the Bolshoi first came to Covent Garden; only now it was a wraith of what it had been then. Extraordinary to find that the Bolshoi's Duke of Courland had become a lay figure, whereas the Royal Ballet's Duke nowadays (at least as interpreted by Derek Rencher) is the sort of bluff, distinctive personality that used to seem so characteristically Bolshoi, and that the Hilarion, once so strongly drawn and so sympathetic, had also dwindled to a mere cog in the story's machinery.

The *Giselle* was sad because it indicated an anaemia—not an effort, good or bad, to make changes but a loss of conviction and, therefore, of vitality. Wrong, though, to deduce that the failings in the *Swan Lake* were only those of bad choreography; for there was a common denominator to the unsatisfactoriness of both ballets. In both we saw classical choreography, whether new-fangled-Grigorovich or ascribed to Petipa and Ivanov, sloppily performed. Sloppily performed it was by soloists and corps de ballet—judged by the Bolshoi's previous standards or by the present as well as past standards of the Royal Ballet.

This, I agree, needs to be qualified. Bessmertnova, a dullish Odette-Odile, was a fine Giselle, a natural for the role, though she, too, was bedevilled by the production's general slackness. Adirchayeva, as Odette-Odile, was painstaking—not sloppy—but badly lacked ballerina-presence. Maximova's Giselle was not to be judged by the half-performance I saw; she retired at half-time, whether because of injury or of fatigue, but at least her first act, though under-engined, had charm. Lavrovsky, as Albrecht and Siegfried, and also as the Nutcracker Prince, had class—an artist as well as a leaping virtuoso; and Vassiliev, though his acting of Albrecht was minimal and though the role seemed to cage rather than liberate his dynamic agility, contributed a breath-taking moment or two. There are also those who greatly admired Alexander Bogatyrov as Siegfried, finding in him an easy elegance and *ballon* which recalled Fadeyechev of yester-year. I confess I found him mannered and marshmallow-soft; I grant the elegance and *ballon* but the general impression, on me, was of Bolshoi-camp rather than Bolshoi-princely.

Then there was *Spartacus*. An extreme contrast. For my part, I had loved it in 1969 and loved it again now, because it shares with —and, thanks to its absurdly, impeccably, ideological scenario, even slightly outdoes—*The Fountain of Bakhchisarai* as a supreme speci-men of what the Bolshoi does best. Take it or leave it, there it is, an elephant of ham dramatics, reiterated, simple pyrotechnics (huge leaps by the men and amazing lifts in the pas-de-deux) and, especially in the choral movements, incredible banalities; and it is well matched by the hammer-blows of Khatchaturian's thumping score. It is awful, and wonderful; but, to me at least, no less wonderful than in 1969, and no more awful; and done with, apparently, just as much ingenuous conviction as before. No company outside Russia could, or would want to imitate it; and I do not know that, even in the Bolshoi, it will stand up to much cast-changing. At the Coliseum it needed Liepa, as the Roman villain, Crassus; when Akimov replaced him there was a distinct loss of force. Timofeyeva, matronly nowadays in shape if not in (simulated) erotic action, was more replaceable (by Adirchayeva) as the Roman villainess. But with Liepa, Maximova and, above and beyond all, Vassiliev, its impact was still huge; so I and nearly all the audience thought.

The 'Don Q' was, we were told, mainly Gorsky's—not much amended since 1940; so it was the oldest of the five productions. But, whether because we were misinformed about its truth-to-Gorsky or because Gorsky of the Tsarist Bolshoi was, as we know, much less elegantly classical than the Maryinsky's Petipa and Ivanov, it gave licence—as *Giselle* and *Swan Lake* did not—to that loosely-knit, off-classical virtuosity in which the Soviet-Bolshoi specializes. And it was well done, though, apart from its two principals, no better than, say, Nureyev's production, as performed last year by the Australians at the Coliseum. Frankly, I would not, as a rule, give you tuppence for this old warhorse of a ballet; but when Maximova is the adorable coquettish Kitri and Vassiliev her Basilio (or Basil) it is another matter. Without them the Bolshoi's 'Don Q' would, I think, be as tedious as any other, but with them there is real excitement between the Minkus-induced yawns. I thought they did the final pas-de-deux (still the one worthy survivor from all this repetitive, pseudo-Spanish, pseudo-gypsy carry-on) only a little less superbly than at Covent Garden five years ago.

The Nutcracker was betwixt and between. Like Spartacus and Swan Lake it was a remake by the Bolshoi's artistic director, Grigoro-vich (in 1966); and it was already known in London. As a pro-duction which takes a single idea and sticks to it it deserves high marks. Of any production I know it is the one which tries most comprehensively, and successfully, to suggest that it is by children for children—and this despite the fact that, at the Coliseum, there was not a child in its cast. This approach to the muddled fairy-tale I like very much and, elsewhere, I have praised—if anything, over-praised—the Bolshoi for it. Maximova and Vassiliev were, again, splendid; and Lavrovsky's 'class' and Sorokina's effortless elevation made a second visit worthwhile. Drosselmeyer (whether Levashev or Simachev) was a kind, eccentric uncle rather than frightening magician—an epitome of Grigorovich's whole approach to the work. But, for these blessings, what a price there was to pay—in the dull-ness of the choreography's classical pastiche (mere strumming, some of it) and in the vulgarity of some of the details (that woolly lamb in the 'pastorale'!) And then the decor. About the decor in any of the five productions I have said nothing as yet and now I shall only say that it was shoddiest in The Nutcracker but shoddy too, in the other four. Not old-fashioned or 'popular', just shoddy.

The best of ballet companies have their bad times. And it would be nice to think that no more than that was wrong with the Bolshoi as we saw it here in 1974—and that, anyway, it was put off its stroke by the demonstrations against it, outside and, to a very small extent, inside the theatre. But such explanations would, I fear, explain too little. The miracle of Soviet ballet (and of the Bolshoi in particular, since Soviet policy exalted it to pride of place over the Kirov) used to be that, notwithstanding the blight of Socialist Realism and Marxist-Leninism and all that was deadly to creative-ness in ballet as in other arts, the tradition of the training lived on grandly in the ballet schools. The Soviet ballets themselves might lack taste and inventiveness but at least the dancers were magnificent. Magnificent not only in the vulgar, Titanesque vigour of the specifically Soviet works (*Spartacus*, *Bakhchisarai*) but, because of their iron-clad tradition of training, magnificent also in the classics. The excellence seemed limitless: ballerinas galore, a wealth of fine soloists and corps de ballet peerless in their meticulous devotion—every member at once a perfectly drilled unit and a passionate believer in the 'vocation'; and the men, especially the leading men, were even more marvellous than the girls.

What seems to have happened now is that the classical standards have become badly eroded. Well, some people did say long ago that the schizophrenic split in Soviet ballet could not persist indefinitely; that split being between the marvellous training of the dancers, on the one hand, and, on the other, the wasteland of Soviet choreography, itself a small corner of the wider wasteland of orthodox Soviet art. The dancers, it was said, must ultimately become as good or as bad as the new choreography which they were required to perform. So if Soviet standards of choreography—and, indeed, the whole Soviet view of ballet—did not change, there was bound to be a change in the standards of Soviet dancing. That, it seems, has happened. It seems that the Bolshoi is now really good only in a *Spartacus* and that its performance of the classics has gone to pot. I have, I am sure, made it amply clear that I for one, have greatly enjoyed *Spartacus*, but I want no more monsters of its kind, or at least very few and very seldom. For *Spartacus* is a caricature and a degenerate hybrid; a caricature of classicism, a hybrid of balletic virtuosity and of that other kind of classical purity—the one demonstrated by the gorgeous Soviet acrobats. It is still done with conviction—yes; but I wonder if even it, and its like, can long remain immune to the lassitude so noticeable now in those ballets which were the source of the Bolshoi's previous strength.

A *Spartacus* or *Bakhchisarai* may long have been the Bolshoi's special thing, but it was the classics, and the training for them, which made the dancers. If a remake of *Swan Lake* is lacklustre choreography danced without distinction and showing a lot of technical weakness and if a *Giselle* is a tired relic of what was once a most vivid production, those, I fear, are signs of a creeping corrosion, much more than the acrobatics, energy and banalities of *Spartacus* are a sign of health. If you can no longer believe in *Giselle*, how can you, in the cynical, sceptical Soviet Union, seventy years after the Revolution, believe much longer in *Spartacus*? And if the

Bolshoi itself comes to realize that it is at its best only in its worst ballets, or at least in balletic monstrosities, what then? Perhaps it will continue to be saved as, when all is said and done, it was saved at the Coliseum, by a Maximova and a Vassiliev. Perhaps it will somehow pick itself up. Or perhaps the politically down-graded Kirov, with its not quite dead Maryinsky tradition and its healthy proneness to defection, will be Soviet ballet's saviour. At all events the time has come for our own ballet to put away the last shreds of its humility. Anyone who, this July, went to the Coliseum and to Covent Garden, will know what I mean.

Index